Margaret Simpson
Illustrated by Philip Reeve

SCHOLASTIC

Published in the UK by Scholastic Children's Books, 2020
Euston House, 24 Eversholt Street, London, NW1 1DB
A division of Scholastic Limited

London ~ New York ~ Toronto ~ Sydney ~ Auckland
Mexico City ~ New Delhi ~ Hong Kong

First published in the UK under the title
Dead Famous: Cleopatra and her Angry Asp
by Scholastic Ltd, 2000

Text copyright © Margaret Simpson, 2000
Illustrations copyright © Philip Reeve, 2000

ISBN 978 1407 19807 1

Page layout services provided by Quadrum Solutions Ltd, Mumbai, India
Printed and bound in the UK by CPI Ltd, Croydon, CR0 4YY

Papers used by Scholastic Children's Books are made from woods grown
in sustainable forests.

2 4 6 8 10 9 7 5 3 1

www.scholastic.co.uk

CONTENTS

INTRODUCTION

Cleopatra was the last queen of Egypt. She died over two thousand years ago, but she'll always be horribly famous! From Roman times everybody has had something to say about her. . .

SHE WAS A FLIRT AND A VAMP AND SHE PINCHED ALL OUR BEST MEN!

SHE KILLED HERSELF FOR LOVE WITH AN ASP!

GORGEOUS FIGURE, SEXY MAKE-UP, REAL STAR QUALITY!

SCRIPT

Screenplay: CLEOPA by Edgar Z Turgleborg Jr.

Wrong! Cleopatra was nothing special to look at – she was a bit short and fat – but she was dead clever. She spoke nine languages, wrote books, and made her country very rich. But most of all she managed to survive her own family – they were horribly famous for the way they murdered each other!

When she came to the throne she was only 19! She ruled for 21 years with the help of two well-chosen boyfriends – the VPRs (Very Powerful Romans) Julius Caesar and Mark Antony. But probably the greatest love of her life was her country, Egypt. Find out about the Cleo who was a brave, brilliant, ruthless ruler – and, yes, rich and sexy with it.

In the end Cleo found herself with no VPR to protect her. She decided she would rather die than live a Roman prisoner, so she dressed up in her best frock and crown, and killed herself. . .

BUT THAT COMES RIGHT AT THE END OF THE BOOK. MASSES OF DEAD INTERESTING, DEAD SCARY AND DEAD EXCITING THINGS HAPPENED TO ME ON THE WAY TO BEING DEAD

Get the Asp Facts on wild and weird Egyptian life, and find out the Roman point of view in the pages of *The Centurion*. Read the writing on the wall with Egyptian graffiti and sneak a peek at Cleo's secret diary. Soon you'll really know all about clever Cleo and her Egyptian asp.

ASP FACT

What's an asp?
An asp is a snake – an Egyptian cobra. A golden, hooded cobra rose up from the crowns of many of the Egyptian gods – and the crowns of the kings of Egypt. Cleo made sure she always wore an asp crown on big state occasions.

Why an asp?
No one's absolutely sure, but the kings of Ancient Egypt were supposed to have all sorts of magical powers – including the ability to tame and charm snakes. A spitting cobra on the crown was a good way of reminding enemies that the snake was on the king's side. Scary!

MEET THE ANCESTORS

Cleopatra was queen of Egypt – but she wasn't really Egyptian. Her family name was Ptolemy – and the Ptolemies came from Macedonia, which is now part of Greece. Actually, Cleo's family had lived in Egypt for three hundred years, but to Egyptians, that was nothing. They were still new kids on the block.

Egypt had been a great civilization for thousands of years before Cleo came along. The Egyptian pharaohs or kings had built the pyramids and huge, mysterious temples to their gods as far back as 3000 BC – maybe even earlier. They weren't short of dosh. Egypt was the richest country in the world, and the centre of a vast empire.

I THINK IT'S TIME WE BUILT ANOTHER MYSTERIOUS TEMPLE... AND THIS ONE CAN BE **REALLY BIG!**

However, from about 1000 BC the pharaohs of Egypt grew weak. First the Assyrians, then the Parthians conquered them. And by 330 BC another great civilization was conquering the world – the Greeks.

The Greeks were led by one of the most famous generals in history – Alexander the Great. Alexander loved fighting and conquering. He did nothing else. Egypt was only one of the countries he conquered, but it was his greatest prize. The kings of Egypt might be weak, but Egypt was still a rich country.

The Greek conquerors were pretty keen to get their hands on the wealth. They also pinched some religious ideas from the ancient Egyptians. In particular, they latched on to the Egyptian idea of god-kings.

Egyptian gods and goddesses

The Egyptians had hundreds of gods and goddesses. Here are four of the most important:

Ra was the sun-god, the daddy of them all, being father of all the Pharaohs. He had a falcon's head on a human body, around which was the sun, and that sacred asp which spat flames to kill off his enemies. One legend said he was born as a child every morning and died as an old man every night.

Osiris and **Isis** were twins, the children of the Sky and the Earth. They fell in love with each other even before they were born and when they grew up they married.

Osiris was top Good Guy, and his brother Seth, who was a Baddy, hated him so much that he killed him and cut him up into little pieces. That's why Osiris is known as the God of the Dead. He is usually shown wrapped up

as a mummy wearing a white crown and carrying a sceptre and flail (a tool used for threshing grain).

Isis – who was top goddess – was devastated when Osiris was killed. With the help of the medicine god, Thoth, she managed to find all the bits of her dead husband and put everything back together – apart from his dangly bits. However she was so powerful she still managed to have a child with her dead husband. Isis wore horns and a sun on her head, and beautiful robes. There were great festivals every year in her honour. She was goddess of the harvest. Cleo just loved dressing up as Isis.

Horus was the son of Isis and so people said he was Osiris come back to life. He ruled with his mother. He also had a falcon-head. People muddled him with a different Horus, the great god of the sky, but that just made him more powerful.

Kings with no name

The ancient Egyptians believed that their kings were descended from these gods. Of course, a bit of them knew it wasn't true and that their kings were really ordinary men. They got round that by saying that when the king put on all his kingly gear (which was a bit like being crowned) the spirit of Horus entered him. That way he became a god living in a human body. He was sacred from then on – so sacred that he couldn't be called by his name. He was called the *per-ao* which we pronounce Pharaoh. It means 'The Royal House'. It's a bit like saying 'The White House' today, meaning the President of America.

The Pharaoh's co-ruler, or queen, was the goddess Isis. In practice she was usually the king's sister!

Alexander the Great

NOW WHAT SHALL I CALL MYSELF? ALEXANDER THE BRILLIANT? ALEXANDER THE FABBY? ALEXANDER THE DISHY? OOH! I KNOW! ALEXANDER THE GREAT!!

After he had conquered Egypt, Alexander went to consult the oracle to the Egyptian sun-god, Ra. Oracles were supposed to be places where the god spoke and answered questions. They were usually in temples or caves. This one was at Siwa, an oasis in the desert.

Consulting oracles was all the rage in both Greece and Egypt. It was a bit like going to see a fortune-teller today, only more serious. The oracle gave you an answer, usually in the voice of the priest who looked after the oracle.

Alexander declared himself King of Egypt. To celebrate he founded a new city at the mouth of the river Nile, which he named Alexandria. This was nothing new. He left an Alexandria in every country he conquered. You can see he was the modest type! By the time he died there were 29 cities called Alexandria!

The Alexandria in Egypt is the most famous of all. Poor old Alexander never lived to see it. He went off to war again and was dead by the time it was built – but it was a posh city. It had big wide streets and grand public buildings. This is where Cleopatra grew up, two hundred years after Alexander, when it was home to several hundred thousand people from all over the world. It was a busy, exciting port, with lots of traders, shops, entertainments – and criminals.

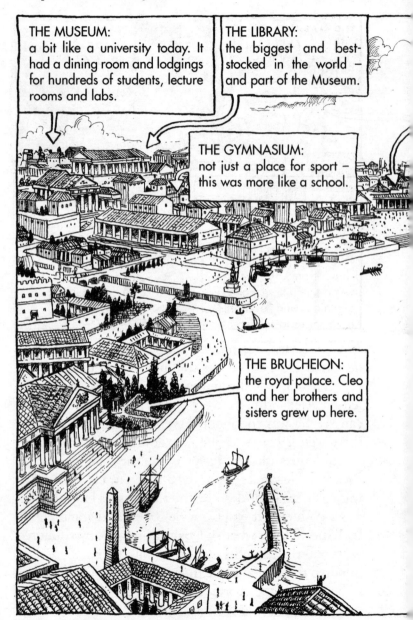

THE MUSEUM:
a bit like a university today. It had a dining room and lodgings for hundreds of students, lecture rooms and labs.

THE LIBRARY:
the biggest and best-stocked in the world – and part of the Museum.

THE GYMNASIUM:
not just a place for sport – this was more like a school.

THE BRUCHEION:
the royal palace. Cleo and her brothers and sisters grew up here.

THE MARKET:
sold everything from food and cloth to make-up and toys.

PHAROS LIGHTHOUSE:
one of the seven wonders of the ancient world. A huge tower on an island across from the harbour, with a fire burning at its top which could be seen for over 30 miles out to sea. An hydraulic pump hoisted the fuel for the fire to the top of the 450 foot tower.

THE HEPTASTADION:
causeway leading from the city to the island of Pharos.

THE GREAT HARBOUR:
ships from all over the world put in here, carrying anything and everything from spices to soldiers.

After Alexander

Alexander the Great was only 33 when he died. He had conquered just about everywhere there was to conquer. Every year he had led his men in months of marching, fighting, then more marching in harsh conditions. He had even marched his men right over the Himalaya mountains into India! Maybe he died of exhaustion.

The moment he died, all his generals began scrambling to grab bits of his huge empire. It was Ptolemy, a Macedonian general, and a real bruiser, who managed to grab Egypt.

Ptolemy and his successors never bothered to learn the language of the Egyptian people, but like Alexander, they were quick to latch on to the idea of god-kings. Of course, the trouble with being a god-king was you couldn't marry an ordinary woman. You needed a god-queen and god-queens could only be found within the family. So, like the pharaohs before them, the Ptolemies married their sisters.

Their Greek relations were very shocked by this. When Ptolemy II married his sister, a Greek poet called Sotades told him he'd done a wicked thing. Ptolemy II thought this was cheeky. He had Sotades shut up in a wooden box and drowned at sea.

Not only did the Ptolemies marry their sisters – they called most of their sons Ptolemy and most of their daughters Cleopatra. So every few years, Ptolemy married Cleopatra, and produced children called Ptolemy and Cleopatra, which must have made home life pretty confusing.

The Cleopatra we're interested in – the famous one – had an older sister called Cleopatra and two little brothers called Ptolemy, as well as two other sisters *not* called Cleopatra. Confused? You will be!

Keeping it in the family

The reason the Ptolemies married their sisters (or sometimes their stepmothers or stepdaughters!) was that they thought it was the best way to be safe from attack.

Wrong! All it meant was the danger came from inside the family. Brothers and sisters, mothers and sons, fathers and daughters ruled jointly – till they fell out, which they always did. Then, more often than not, the row ended in murder! The Ptolemies were always killing each other off. And our Cleopatra was no exception.

The early Ptolemies didn't stand any nonsense. They were tough soldiers who kept the Egyptians in order. But over time, life in Egypt turned them soft and fat. One of the later Ptolemies, Ptolemy VIII was so gross that he needed two servants, one on each side, to support him as he walked.

In 80 BC the wife (and stepmother!) of another Ptolemy – Ptolemy XI – died a mysterious death. The Alexandrian mob reckoned he'd murdered her. They didn't like him much anyway, so this gave them an excuse to kill him. There were no children, so now they had to look round quickly for a new king. They chose the son of an earlier Ptolemy. This man took the name of Ptolemy XII and married – guess who? – his sister, Cleopatra.

MEET THE FAMILY

This new Ptolemy and his sister Cleopatra were our Cleopatra's mum and dad.

The Ptolemies always chose posh names for themselves to tag on to Ptolemy. They would call themselves things like 'Saviour' or 'Shown-by-God'. Cleopatra's dad called himself 'the New Dionysus'.

The wild and wacky god of wine

Dionysus was the wild Greek god of wine, women and song. We know that Cleo's dad was musical, because another of his nicknames was Auletes, the Flute-Player. He also had a reputation for getting drunk and doing rude and cruel things, so maybe Dionysus was the right name for him.

Whatever the Ptolemies called themselves, the people of Alexandria didn't go along with any god nonsense. They knew who Cleo's dad was. They'd grown up with him. They called him Nothos. It's – oo-er – a rude word. It meant his mum and dad were never married.

As for Cleo's mum, we know almost nothing about her. She disappears from the history books around the same time Cleo was born. She may have been bumped off, or maybe she died in childbirth. Auletes, the flute-player, didn't marry again but he had three more children after Cleo's mother died.

CLEOPATRA THEA - THE THIRD CHILD AND OUR CLEOPATRA. KEPT HER HEAD DOWN AND HER NOSE IN A BOOK WHILE HER SISTERS SLUGGED IT OUT.

PTOLEMY - FIFTH IN THE FAMILY AND FIRST BOY. DESTINED TO MARRY WHICHEVER OF HIS SISTERS WOUND UP QUEEN... EVEN THOUGH TRYPHAENA WAS OLD ENOUGH TO BE HIS MUM.

PTOLEMY - THE BABY OF THE FAMILY.

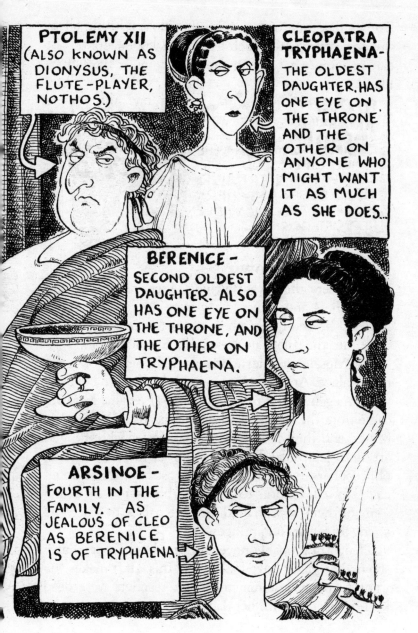

21

Every single one of Cleo's brothers and sisters died in the power struggles which left Cleopatra queen, so you can imagine what life in the nursery must have been like!

A class of her own

After nursery, there was no going to school for Cleo and her brothers and sisters. They were far too important. Instead, she and her brothers and sisters had tutors who came into the palace in Alexandria to teach them.

The Museum in Alexandria was right next door to the royal palace. And the Museum was *the* place to be if you were an egghead in Ptolemaic times. The name Museum came from the Greek word which means 'House of the Muses' and the Muses were the goddesses who inspired art and learning. This Museum attracted scholars, philosophers, mathematicians and astronomers, who all came to Alexandria to be brain-boxes together, and some of them were invited into the palace to teach the young princesses and princes.

Cleopatra probably never had a school report, but if she had, it might have looked like this. (If it makes you want to puke, just remember her teachers were dead keen to keep in with her dad. . .)

SCHOOL REPORT
CLEOPATRA THEA (AGE 7)

GREEK	Completely brilliant. Cleopatra Thea reads and writes exquisitely.
LATIN	OPTIMA!
ARAMAIC	How can I convey the talent of the tiny princess?
HEBREW	Noble king, you have given birth to the most brilliant prodigy. Only one as wonderful as yourself could have produced such a child.
PHOENICIAN	Words fail! Already Her Highness speaks the Phoenician language fluently.
MATHEMATICS	Excellent. The young princess shows real talent in calculating interest rates.
SCIENCE	Cleopatra Thea is another jewel in the Ptolemy crown. Such intelligence! Such an inventive mind! Such understanding of astronomy! Such interest in Geometry!
DRAMA	Excellent. Cleopatra is a natural. She shows a talent for dominating any scene. A true princess.

Maybe her teachers were exaggerating a bit to please her royal father, but one thing is certain – Cleopatra *was* a real egg-head who seems to have been interested in everything. When she grew up she is said to have written books on weights and measures; gynaecology (medical know-how about women's reproductive systems); alchemy, which was a mix of chemistry and magic; and make-up. And, of course, there were all those languages she spoke.

In fact, the whole family was clever. The Ptolemies may have been cruel, incompetent rulers but they loved art, music and learning. They shipped books over from Athens in Greece, and by Cleopatra's time the library at Alexandria contained more than half a million books in the form of scrolls and papyri.

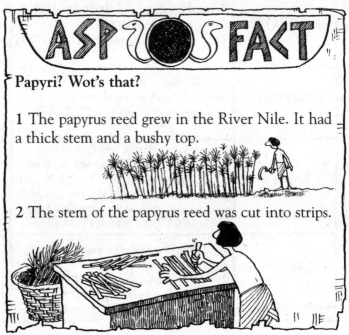

ASP FACT

Papyri? Wot's that?

1 The papyrus reed grew in the River Nile. It had a thick stem and a bushy top.

2 The stem of the papyrus reed was cut into strips.

3 The strips were laid side by side.

4 Then more strips were laid horizontally across the first layer.

5 A big weight was put on them, and the sap leaked out and glued them together to form a single piece of papyrus.

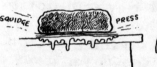

SQUIDGE   PRESS

AND HERE'S ONE I MADE EARLIER!

One sheet was called a papyrus; more than one were called papyri.

The Egyptians used papyrus reeds for making everything from fishing nets and string to river rafts. Thin reeds were used for string. Thick reeds were sliced so that they looked like planks of wood and used to make rafts or boats. In fact there were a hundred and one uses for papyrus reeds.

The Nile was the centre of Egyptian life. Egyptians fished the river, they hunted animals and trapped birds in the marshes – and they went out on it for parties. If the young Cleo had kept a diary, she might have described a day like this:

CLEOPATRA'S SECRET DIARY
(AGED 10)

Big excitement! This week we went hunting on the river. And our Divine Father came too! It is the first time that DF has come along on a children's picnic for ages. There were about forty of us altogether, what with father's mates and the slaves.

The river is high after the rain but Archelaeus, the new drop-dead gorgeous young tutor, says it may still not be enough for a good harvest. He says the rise of the river depends not on our rain but on the snows far away on the mountains of Ethiopia. Tryph says he's talking rubbish. She says no one believes that, but I think he may be right.

DF says that we must pray to the gods that the river goes on rising. I find that a bit muddling. Does it mean we pray to DF? I mean, he's a god. That's why we always have to call him DF. But if he is a god, why does he need to pray? Or why do we, come to that? He can see what's happening. Why doesn't he just send more rain? I asked Tryph, but she only laughed.

'Isn't she sweet?' she said to Archelaeus — she was flirting with him the whole time. 'She still believes it.'

Archelaeus looked dead worried. He was scared someone might overhear. But no one was listening. DF had drunk a lot of wine by this time and all his mates were crowded round, begging him to play his flute.

'Believes what, Tryph?' I said. I knew what she meant, of course, I just wanted to make her say what I know she thinks — that DF isn't divine at all.

She didn't answer. So I went on pestering her to wind her up. In the end she gave me one of her most poisonous smiles and said that if it was as simple as praying to DF we would never have had these years of drought and bad harvests. I pretended I didn't know what she meant. I'd got Arsinoe going by this time and she kept saying, 'What do you mean?' as well.

Tryph was ready to strangle us both. She told us to go for a swim, and when I said I didn't want to, she pinched my arm hard. She wanted me out of the way so she could go on flirting with poor Archelaeus. Who really likes me best, because I'm more fun than Tryph. And cleverer.

← TRYPH — yuk, boo!

YOURS TRULY— FUN, CLEVER, PRETTY, MODEST ETC. ETC. →

Next thing I know Tryph was calling over another raft, and ordering the eunuch[1] Pothinus to swim with us. I hate Pothinus. He is a young, fat man who's always sucking up to important people. He <u>hates</u> swimming and he's terrified of crocodiles. I looked at Arsinoe, and we both grinned. Suddenly, making Pothinus swim seemed much more fun than winding up Tryph.

By this time DF had got in on the act. He had heard we wanted to swim, and he told Pothinus to do as he was told. Pothinus began to sweat and shake. He pretended to be really worried that the crocodiles would swallow 'our sweet divine princesses'. Which was complete rubbish, because

SCAREDY POT

[1]Eunuchs were men who had an operation on their private parts so that they would be trusted around the women of the court.

he can't stand me and Arsinoe. He's completely besotted with the two little Ptolemies.

DF can see through him as well as I can. He told him it was because of the sweet divine princesses that he wanted Pothinus in the water first. He was bait, said DF. If no crocs appeared, we would know it was safe for us. Pothinus was practically in tears, but that just made DF more cruel. He was completely drunk by this time. **SWIM!** he roared to Pothinus.

And so the fat freak had to jump into the deep, dark waters of the river. He swam round and round in circles, looking over his shoulder. Then someone gave me a shove from behind. Tryph, of course. I toppled into the water on top of Pothinus. It was cold after the brilliant heat of the sun, and I didn't enjoy it much. I'm scared of crocodiles too! Luckily there weren't any, and when everyone saw we were safe, they joined us in the water, until only the slaves were left on deck, looking hot and envious.

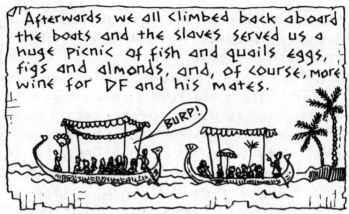

Afterwards we all climbed back aboard the boats and the slaves served us a huge picnic of fish and quails eggs, figs and almonds, and, of course, more wine for DF and his mates.

BURP!

OK, so this particular picnic never happened. But the rich families did have days out on boats down the Nile. And Ptolemy the Flute-Player was definitely a drunk and cruel man who enjoyed humiliating people by forcing them to do things they didn't want to do.

ASP FACT

Chomp chomp, you're dead

There were hundreds of crocodiles in the Nile. For centuries the Egyptians had thought this was a great way to get rid of their enemies. They'd throw them, dead or alive, to the crocodiles. There were no bodies to bury, so it was all very ecological.

SEE YOU LATER, AGITATOR!

IN A NILE CROCODILE!

Lotsa different letters

The writing from Ancient Egypt was more like pictures than writing. The signs are called 'hieroglyphs' which means 'sacred writing'. They were sometimes grouped together in boxes called 'cartouches'. Cartouches were carved on temple walls and stone pillars called steles.

Then there was hieratic writing, which was quicker to write. This was for notes and unofficial messages.

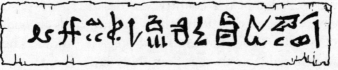

Cleo would have written a diary in Greek – which looks like this.

ΚΛΕΟΠΑΤΡΑ

Two hundred years ago an archaeologist found a piece of stone with the same thing written on it three times over – in hieroglyphs, hieratic and Greek. He could understand Greek, and so he was able to work out what each sign in the other languages stood for. From that people learnt to read all the other cartouches.

You can see that piece of stone if you go to the British Museum in London. It's called the Rosetta Stone.

31

BAD HARVESTS AND BIG NEIGHBOURS

In some ways, Egypt in Cleo's day was quite like Egypt today. A lot of the country was desert. However, the desert held a secret. Beneath its shifting sands lay oodles of boodle – gold, minerals and precious stones. These were as valuable then as they are today.

The mighty river

There was one long strip of Egypt which was green and fertile: the Nile Valley. The Nile is a very long river running right through the middle of Egypt. It gathers water from the mountains of Ethiopia and central Africa and flows all the way to the Mediterranean Sea. A big dam was built this century, but before that the river flooded every spring, making the Nile even more massive. The water spread for miles. When it drained away, it left behind a rich black silt in which everything grew well.

The Egyptians had farmed this long, rich valley for thousands of years, since the time of the Pharaohs and before. They had become very good at it. They built canals to take the water away from the river and wet more land. And all along the river, far south into what is known as 'Upper Egypt', there were villages, cities and temples. There weren't many Greeks here. These people had been Egyptian for generations.

Either side of the river, neat parcels of land were marked off like patchwork. Tall stones marked the boundary between one farmer's land and another's. When the floods came, only the stones could be seen above the water.

In good years, the Egyptians could grow anything – and they did. They grew all sorts of grains, and made lots of different kinds of bread, biscuits and cake. (They also had bad teeth because the flour was ground by hand and had grit in it which broke their teeth or wore down their enamel.) They grew flax for linen cloth and linseed oil. They grew grapes for wine and grazed cattle for milk, meat and leather. They also grew all sorts of other fruits and vegetables, so they had a pretty good diet.

But everything depended on the river rising to the right height. Too low, and not enough land flooded. Too high, and the floodwater swept away the irrigation channels which kept the land watered throughout the hot summer months.

I grew it, it's mine

The country farmers along the Nile were very happy to sail down river and sell their produce to the cities when harvests were good. In bad years they weren't so keen. They wanted to keep the food they had grown to feed their own families.

ASP FACT

Nilometers
The government kept track of how much the river rose. Every little town along the river had its 'Nilometer'. These looked like wells, or sometimes steps. The floodwater flowed into them. The king's tax collectors looked to see where the high water mark was. From that they knew how much land was fertile and how much of his crop the farmer could afford to give the king.

THAT'LL BE 50% THIS YEAR

THAT'S NOT FAIR!

THAT'S LAST YEAR'S MARK!

I DON'T KNOW WHY THE KING NEEDS IT ALL ANYWAY...

HE SELLS IT, DOESN'T HE!

The big city

There were towns all along the River Nile, but the biggest was the city of Alexandria, right at the mouth of the Nile.

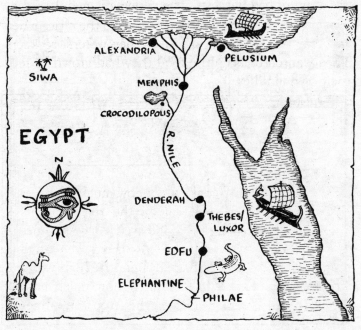

Alexandria was the capital of Ptolemaic Egypt. A bit like London or New York today, it was a lively place, full of people from all over the world. In particular there were a lot of Greek people whose ancestors had arrived with the Ptolemies. There was also a big Jewish colony – and there were always merchants and sailors arriving from Rome and Cyprus and other countries in the Middle East. Just like today, the people who lived in the big city were a streetwise lot, who took what their leaders told them with a big pinch of salt.

35

Food prices were high in the city, and when harvests were bad, food was scarce. This made the city-dwellers very stroppy indeed.

During the reign of Ptolemy the Flute-Player, there was a run of bad harvests. The people blamed the king.

A shortage of food was only one of Ptolemy the Flute-Player's problems. He had another problem, which was just as serious – if not more so.

Meet the enemy

From the time of the Pharaohs, Egypt had been the envy of her neighbours. With all that rich farm land around the river Nile, plus her mineral resources, she was the richest country in the world. Other countries wanted to conquer her. They wanted all that wealth.

By the time of the Ptolemies, another powerful empire was growing up: the Roman Empire, which would one day span the whole of Europe and most of the Middle East, including Judaea, the land of the Jews.

By the time of Ptolemy Auletes, the Roman Empire was huge and controlled by its three most powerful generals. Julius Caesar, Pompey antd Crassus were known as the Triumvirs. They shared all the best perks between them.

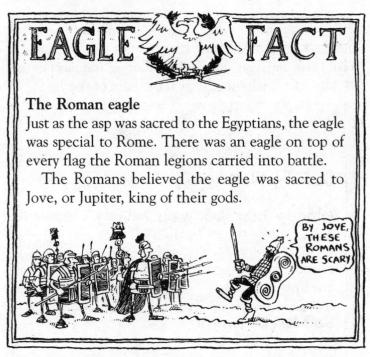

The Roman eagle

Just as the asp was sacred to the Egyptians, the eagle was special to Rome. There was an eagle on top of every flag the Roman legions carried into battle.

The Romans believed the eagle was sacred to Jove, or Jupiter, king of their gods.

Even though they had more lands than they could keep in order, Roman rulers still liked conquering other countries. It gave them something to do. And they particularly liked the look of rich Egypt. They thought all that dosh would go a long way to paying their thousands of soldiers.

Cleo's dad was scared they would march in and depose him. He was even more scared that his people would rise up and kick him out. Either way, he would be out on his ear.

He knew he couldn't win over his people so he sucked up to the Roman rulers. When Cleo was ten he wrote a letter to the Roman Triumvirs. It probably went something like this:

The Brucheion Palace

In the eighth month of the twenty-first year of the reign of king Ptolemy XII[1]

Dear Noble Ones,

Glad to hear your great military campaigns have all gone so well.

If I didn't know how much work it is running a kingdom, I'd think you'd be finding life a bit quiet now you've won all your battles. As it is, I know you must be busy keeping all those Picts and Celts and Jews and Germans and Gauls in order. It must be a relief to know there's a guy like me around, so there's one country at least you don't have to worry about. No fear of Egypt attacking Rome while I'm king! You can be sure of that!

I wonder if you could do me a favour! Harvests haven't been too good here recently, and the people are a bit restless — you know what they're like,

[1] 59 BC to us. The Romans counted time from the founding of their city. Their year 1 we call 753 BC. (To save ourselves getting in a muddle, we'll include the dating system we understand.)

always ready to blame their rulers when things go wrong. It would really strengthen my position if they knew you backed me.

Your loyal servant,

the eternally grateful and peace-loving

Ptolemy XII Dionysus

THE CAPITOL, ROME
X/IX/DCXCV[1]

DEAR PTOLEMY,

MANY THANKS FOR YOUR PROMISE OF LOYALTY. PLEASE SEND US 6000 TALENTS AND WE WILL BE HAPPY TO ISSUE A PROCLAMATION ALONG THE LINES YOU SUGGEST.

WE LOOK FORWARD TO YOUR EARLY REPLY.

EVER YOURS,

JULIUS, POMPEY, AND CRASSUS
TRIUMVIRS OF THE GREAT ROMAN EMPIRE

Poor Ptolemy Auletes. Six thousand talents was a whole year's income for Egypt. He had no spare cash and he didn't dare try and raise more taxes in case he started a revolution. Instead he borrowed the gold – from a Roman moneylender.

Now he was really in trouble. Moneylenders charged huge interest, so his debt kept increasing. As for the Egyptian people, they didn't give a fig about statements from Rome telling them who was their rightful king. By the end of 59 BC Ptolemy XII needed more than Roman words to keep his throne. There were riots in the streets: the people threw him out and he fled to Rome to ask his 'allies' to send an army to put him back in power. But, of course, he couldn't hop on a plane. He had to go by sea.

Ships in those days carried both oars and sails – sails for when the wind was behind them, and oars for when it wasn't. Not just a couple of oars, either. There were huge banks of oars, one each side of the ship, often with more than one man to an oar. The oarsmen, who were slaves, all pulled together, and the ship made its way into the wind across the choppy Mediterranean Sea.

Because he was running away, it wasn't even a royal ship, so his quarters wouldn't have been very special.

And poo to you too!

On his way to Rome, Ptolemy the Flute-Player put in at the island of Rhodes. He arranged a meeting with a very important visting Roman, Cato the Younger. Like most Romans, he didn't think much of poor, fat, debauched old Ptolemy and decided to show it. He was on the loo when Ptolemy arrived. He deliberately didn't tell his servants to ask the Egyptian King to wait outside.

'Show him in!' he said.

So the King of Egypt was shown in and had to talk business with Cato while Cato continued to do his business.

Poo!

ASP FACT

Keeping track of the time

Egyptians and Romans both had different ways of counting their years. People usually counted time onwards from a Big Event – like the beginning of a new reign. They would say 'in the tenth year of the reign of Ptolemy Soter', for instance – or 'three hundred years after the founding of Rome'.

Actually – we still do the same thing today. The important event from which Western countries count time is the birth of Jesus Christ. Since then no one has succeeded in coming up with a new and even more important event to start time with. (The French tried it in 1792 after their Revolution, but their new calendar just didn't catch on.)

While the cat's away

While Cleo's dad was away in Rome, back in Alexandria all sorts of plots and counterplots were going on. You were not allowed to say openly what you thought under the Ptolemies but people secretly wrote rude things about them on *steles* or upright stone slabs in the city – a bit like graffiti on walls and bridges today.

Here's the story of what happened next – and what the writing on *steles* might have said about it.

Cleopatra Tryphaena declares herself queen. She promises no more bribes to Rome.

NOTHOS WENT AND DID A BUNK
TRYPHAENA MAKES HER PLAY
NO MORE GOLD FOR ROME
SHE SAYS
BUT ROME WON'T GO AWAY...

Cleopatra Tryphaena dies suddenly – no one knows why.

WHO KILLED QUEEN TRYPH?
NOT I, SAID HER DAD
AS HE SAT PLAYING TUNES
IN HIS SMART ROMAN PAD

Berenice is declared the Queen of Egypt.

Messengers sent from Berenice to ask the Roman Triumvirs to recognize her as queen are murdered on the beach. Ptolemy's men have been lying in wait for them.

While all this was going on, the city of Alexandria was in turmoil. Troops loyal to Berenice restored order, but many people were scared to throw in their lot with her in case Ptolemy decided to come back and fight.

They were right to be cautious. In the end, after a lot of dithering, the Romans decided to support Ptolemy the Flute-Player and restore him to his throne – in return for more money, naturally! A Roman general called Gabinius was sent with an army to Alexandria. Ptolemy's moneylender went along too to be sure of getting his interest on the dosh – and so did a hunky young soldier called Mark Antony.

Hearing a Roman army was on its way, the supporters of Berenice were scared stiff. The Romans were much better soldiers than the Egyptians, who knew they didn't have a hope. However, they thought the Queen would be stronger if she had a husband, and so they found a man to marry her. Berenice didn't like him. She thought he was a real oik, so she had him strangled a few days after the wedding.

A second husband was found. He must have been quaking in his sandals. Who was going to get him first,

45

his wife or the Romans? As it turned out, the Romans got him. He died in battle against them. Mark Antony, who was always generous to his enemies, as well as drop-dead gorgeous, gave him a posh funeral. This really annoyed King Ptol. However, Berenice was shown no mercy. She had tried to grab her father's throne so her father had an excuse to execute her – along with all her supporters.

Where was Cleopatra during all this time? No one knows. She was twelve years old when her father left, fourteen when he was returned to power. If she was in Alexandria, her life must often have been in danger, what with all the upheavals, inside and outside the palace. So did her father take her with him to Rome? Was she sent away to another city out of harm's way? Was this how she learned to speak the language of the local Egyptians? Or did she just keep her head down, read books in the vast Alexandrian library and pretend not to be interested in politics? We'll never know.

What we do know is that she survived and that her father named her as his heir when he got back – so if she was in Egypt through all this, she must have steered clear of her sisters' plots.

CLEOPATRA'S SECRET DIARY
(AGED 16)

Have just returned from trip up the Nile with Arsinoe and DF. He said he wanted us to see beyond the city to the great kingdom up the river. What sights we have seen!

Vast barge under sail as we left — wind was blowing from the north. Out of the city, we passed first through marsh, then grazing land, then vineyards where grapes ripened in the blazing sunshine.

Then DF said something that made my heart leap. 'See what a rich country you will one day rule.' So I **am** to be queen. I knew it. I always knew it, though I could never see how. Who could have dreamt that that horrible old Tryph and that maniac Berenice would bring about their own downfall! What a relief they are both dead!

Does Arsinoe feel the same about me as I feel about them? I bet she does. She is always getting in little digs at me. One day she said she thought it was a pity I am not taller, because I would never show off the royal robes to advantage.

Another evening, she started on about how the most powerful queen of Egypt was Arsinoe II. So I pointed out to her that Berenice III had been a powerful queen too, but look what had happened to our sister Berenice. Then I walked away and stood in the prow of the barge. I knew she was watching me with hatred and envy. I shall have to be careful of her.

NOTE: Set spies to watch her.

On the banks, I could see the small fires outside the farmers' houses on the plain spreading out from the river. There were children's voices on the wind, and I felt half-envious of these people who are not burdened with power. I bet they don't fear death from each other as we do.

We sailed a long way south, way past Memphis, where DF said he should have been crowned. I asked him why he wasn't and he said there had been too much unrest in Alexandria — that he didn't dare leave the city.

I realized then that poor DF has been unsure of his throne from the very day he inherited it.

We went on and on, for hundreds of miles. The river narrowed all the time, and finally we came to Denderah,

Where my father has set men to finish the great temple begun by our ancestors. It is a fine, rich building, a monument to the great power of our family.

At a bend in the river we came to a temple of Sobek, the crocodile god. And there on a sandbank lay dozens of crocodiles, sunning themselves. I was scared as we tied up and jumped ashore by the temple in case the crocodiles came after us. A local man told us that they had killed seven people this past month – three grown fishermen, a woman and three children.

At Coptos DF set up an altar to the old Egyptian gods still worshipped by the local people. That night we sat drinking wine aboard the barge, or rather, DF drank wine with Arsinoë. I didn't touch a drop. In my family you need to keep a clear head.

'This is the true Egypt,' said my father that night. 'Alexandria is not Egypt. Alexandria is simply – Alexandria. A busy

49

City, full of mongrel people. Here there are real Egyptians. These are the people who pay their taxes and keep the city fed. You should always make sure these people love you when you are queen.

It seemed a long, long way from Alexandria and the modern world. A timeless place. I saw how my divine father loves old Egypt. How despite his Greek blood he is drawn to the Egyptian people. He was well-pleased when he discovered that I could speak with them in their own language. He said that no ruler from the house of Ptolemy had ever done that before.

On the journey back he spoke of the danger to Egypt from Rome. The need to have the Romans as our allies, even though it cost so much.

I think he is right. We cannot possibly stand up to them, we have to have them on our side. Yet it is such a drain on the country, to bribe and bribe, to borrow in order to bribe — and then pay interest on the bribes.

To keep the Romans on our side without money. That is the challenge. There has to be a way.

There *was* a way, and it wasn't many years before Cleopatra discovered what it was.

QUEEN CLEO

Cleo's dad ruled for four more years. Things didn't get any better for him. His Roman moneylender insisted on being made head of finance for all Egypt. This guy raked off so much money in 'taxes' that the Alexandrian mob set on him.

THIS CAN BE A VERY TAXING JOB!

He barely escaped with his life and had to make a run for it back to Rome. The general Gabinius was no better. He was taking bribes right, left and centre too.

The Romans didn't really mind their people screwing money out of foreigners – provided they gave it all to Rome. These two didn't do that. All the money they took from the Egyptians went into their own pockets. When they went home they found themselves on trial for fraud – against the Romans.

CLEOPATRA'S SECRET DIARY

The ghastly Gabinius has gone home. He's taken Mark Antony with him. Thank goodness for that. MA seems to think that just because he's tall and good-looking I ought to fancy him.

All right, so he is fun. And his men like him. And everyone says he's kind and generous. But he drinks too much, and anyway, I am an Egyptian princess. I'm not going to throw myself at the first handsome Roman soldier I meet. I *must* marry a god-king for the sake of Egypt. Pity it's going to have to be one of my little brothers...

Gabinius has left a whole crew of men behind, to help DF keep order. They don't seem to be keeping order to me. They're forever brawling and causing trouble.

When I'm queen there won't be any Romans keeping me in power.

A Roman army stayed on in Egypt for the rest of Ptolemy's reign. Ptolemy knew the Alexandrians hated him so much that he couldn't manage without it. He had to put up with the fact that he was just a puppet king.

A year before he died he told Cleopatra again that she was to be his heir. What Cleo didn't know was that he had sent some papers to Rome.

THE LAST WILL AND TESTAMENT
OF
PTOLEMY XII DIONYSUS
KING OF ALL EGYPT

I HEREBY LEAVE MY ENTIRE KINGDOM (EGYPT) TO MY DAUGHTER CLEOPATRA THEA AND TO MY ELDER SON PTOLEMY, WHO SHALL MARRY EACH OTHER AND BE KNOWN AS KING PTOLEMY XIII AND QUEEN CLEOPATRA VII.

IF I DIE WHILE MY SAID SON, THE ELDER PTOLEMY, IS STILL A CHILD, I APPOINT THE EUNUCH POTHINUS TO ACT AS HIS GUARDIAN UNTIL HE COMES OF AGE.

THIS WILL IS LODGED WITH THE PUBLIC TREASURY IN ROME. I KNOW THAT THE MOST WONDERFUL, NOBLE ROMAN LEADERS CAN DEFINITELY BE TRUSTED TO CARRY OUT THE WISHES OF THEIR MOST LOYAL ALLY (MYSELF) KNOWING THAT WITH MY BELOVED SON AND DAUGHTER ON THE THRONE, ROME WILL HAVE NO TROUBLE FROM EGYPT.

ΠΤΟΛΕΜΥ

PTOLEMY XII DIONYSUS, ON THE 5th DAY OF THE 3rd MONTH OF THE TWENTY-EIGHTH YEAR OF HIS REIGN

Cleopatra didn't get wind of her dad's will until he died. When she did, she was spitting tacks.

CLEOPATRA'S SECRET DIARY

DF was such a liar! I can say it now he's dead. Liar, liar, liar! I mean, I always knew I'd be lumbered with young Ptol. There's no chance of ditching your kid brother in this country. Things might have been OK. Ptol is only a kid, I could have handled him easily.

But DF has made Pothinus regent!!!! **Pothinus!** How dare he! DF **knew** how much I hate him! And how much the fat freak hates me! He's dangerous. And he's not going to do as he's told. ◊◊◊ OH!!! It's the most frustrating thing of all, to be queen and **still** to have to watch my step. Horrible old DF! I'm lumbered!

Cleopatra was right. She was lumbered. She and little Ptolemy (who was only ten and every bit as irritating as most little brothers) were married and known as the 'Brother-and-Sister-Loving Gods.'

Round one: Wot, no Ptoly?

Married or not, Cleo had no intention of ruling jointly with anyone. Right from the start, while Ptol played games with his little pals in the Palace, Cleo set about showing Pothinus who was boss. She issued a brand-new coin. Instead of having the heads of both the brother-and-sister-loving gods on them, the coins carried Cleopatra's head. Young Ptol just wasn't there.

By the way, Cleo didn't look particularly pretty on her coins. She had a hook nose and a chin that stuck out. It was a strong face with lots of character. We know because some of those coins have survived to this day.

ASP FACT

Money means power

Throughout history, rulers have always shown people who is the power in the land by putting their own picture on coins. This was especially important in times when there were no newspapers and people couldn't read. Every time you paid for something with a coin, you were reminded who was king (or queen).

All through her reign, Cleo issued coins-with-a-message – and so did the Romans.

Round two: The little white bull

Right from the start Cleo was very good at what today would be called photo opportunities. There were no cameras in those days, but rulers knew they could influence the way people thought about them by the things they did, and the way they did them.

CLEOPATRA'S SECRET DIARY.

They tell me that the sacred bull of Buchis is dying. I shall travel up river to Thebes and personally deliver the new young bull to the temple of Hermonthis. This is a perfect opportunity to show the people of Upper Egypt that I am no Greek, but truly an Egyptian queen. DF would be proud of me!!

This is exactly what Cleopatra did. The White Bull of Buchis was very important to the Egyptians. They believed he was the living form of the god Ra. Whenever an old bull died, a new and magnificent young bull had to be found to take his place. Cleopatra went all the way up river to Thebes and rowed the new bull to the temple. We know this because there is a real stele at the temple with the following inscription: 'In the first year of her reign, the Queen, the Father-Loving Goddess, rowed the bull in the barge of Ra to Hermonthis.'

Cleopatra didn't actually row the boat herself. More than likely she wore her most splendid royal robes and sat in state while her slaves did the rowing.

But the message to the people was loud and clear – I am one of you. The people of Upper Egypt liked Cleopatra right from the start.

Round three: Do as you're told!

Back in Alexandria, it was business as usual. Harvests were bad, the people were restless and they blamed the Ptolemies. Cleopatra needed Roman support.

However, the Romans – the same troops left by General Gabinius and Mark Antony – caused more problems than they solved. They were a law unto themselves.

One day a boat, with two young Roman nobles aboard, sailed into Alexandria. They had been sent by their father, the Roman governor in Syria. He needed troops and he had sent for the Gabinians to come and join his army.

The Gabinians didn't want to leave Alexandria. They were having a good time. Many of them had Alexandrian wives and children and they were turned right off by the thought of leaving home and fighting once more. They didn't just tell the young Romans to get lost – they killed them.

For Cleopatra this was a heaven-sent opportunity. She could prove her loyalty to Rome *and* teach the Gabinians who was boss. Very bravely, because it could easily have caused a riot, the young Queen ordered the guilty men to be arrested and sent to the Roman governor in chains.

So far, Cleopatra had outmanoeuvred her little brother and his guardians. She was proving herself a strong and independent queen. However, the following year the harvest was worse than ever. There was no food in the markets and people were starving.

Round four: It's his fault as well

CLEOPATRA'S SECRET DIARY

Pothinus is huffing and puffing again about little Ptol. How I never let him have a look-in. He wants Ptol's name on all government documents. Says I have to stop acting in this 'high-handed manner'.

So for once, I shall give in. The harvest is worse than we thought, and I have to order the farmers to send almost everything they have grown to the city. The country people will hate it and

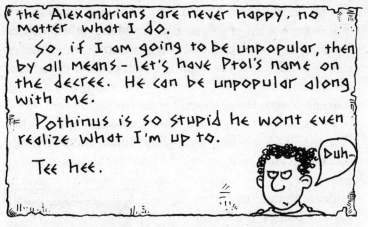

the Alexandrians are never happy, no matter what I do.

So, if I am going to be unpopular, then by all means – let's have Ptol's name on the decree. He can be unpopular along with me.

Pothinus is so stupid he wont even realize what I'm up to.

Tee hee.

Duh–

This is exactly what happened. The farmers in the countryside were ordered to send massive amounts of food to the city. And – for the first time – the decree was signed by Queen Cleopatra and her co-ruler and kid-brother, King Ptolemy XIII.

HA! NOW THE PEOPLE WILL KNOW THAT PTOLEMY IS THEIR KING!

BOO! BOO! DOWN WITH PTOLEMY!

While all this was going on at home, Cleo still had to keep the Romans sweet. The big question was. . .

Which Romans?

For many centuries Rome had been a republic. This meant there were no god-kings in Rome. Instead Rome had a constitution and was supposed to be controlled by a council made up of posh rich Roman citizens called 'the senate'. In practice, the triumvirs (those three powerful soldiers) did what they wanted and more or less ignored the senate, and the rich posh citizens were pretty cross about it.

In any case, there weren't three triumvirs any more. (Crassus was killed in 53 BC in battle against the Parthians.[1]) Now there were only two people who really had power in Rome...

Gnaeus Pompeius
a.k.a. Pompey the Great
Soldier, famous for clearing the Mediterranean Sea of pirates and winning battles. When he saw he was not as powerful as Julius Caesar, he decided he didn't want to be a dictator and said that he believed in the senate system after all.

Julius Caesar
Famous for conquering Gaul (France) and invading Britain. Wrote books while marching with his army. Interested in just about everything – science, art, theatre, warfare – and women. Many thought he wanted to be sole ruler of the Roman Empire.

[1]The Parthians were Persians; they lived in what is now Iran.

By 49 BC, Pompey and Caesar were at war. Caesar's army drove Pompey out of Italy. Pompey fled to Asia Minor, but sent his son to Egypt to demand supplies for his troops. He also wanted all those Romans left by Gabinius to leave Alexandria and join his army. Here's the sort of letter Cleo sent in reply.

THE BRUCHEION PALACE
SIXTH MONTH OF THE SECOND YEAR OF
THE REIGN OF CLEOPATRA AND PTOLEMY
THE BROTHER-AND-SISTER LOVING GODS (49BC)

DEAR POMPEY,
I AM GIVING THIS LETTER TO YOUR SON TO GIVE TO YOU. AS YOU WILL KNOW BY THE TIME YOU RECEIVE IT, I AM DOING EVERYTHING YOU ASKED. YOUR SON IS BRINGING AS MUCH GRAIN AS WE CAN SEND NOW (PLEASE REMEMBER THERE IS A FAMINE HERE) AND ALSO 500 MEN WHO SERVED UNDER GABINIUS.

I REMAIN,
  YOUR LOYAL ALLY

ΚΛΕΟΠΑΤΡΑ

  CLEOPATRA, QUEEN OF EGYPT

How did Cleopatra manage to get the Gabinians to leave Alexandria and fight for Pompey? No one knows. Maybe she bribed them to go. However she did it, Pompey was very pleased.

> ROMAN ARMY CAMP, ASIA MINOR
> YEAR DCCV (49 BC)
>
> DEAR CLEOPATRA AND PTOLEMY,
>
> THANKS FOR THE GRAIN, AND ALSO THE SOLDIERS. YOU HAVE PROVED YOURSELVES GOOD FRIENDS, AND IN THANKS FOR YOUR HELP, I HEREBY APPOINT MYSELF GUARDIAN OF YOUNG PTOLEMY.
>
> ALL THE BEST,
>
> GNAEUS POMPEIUS

Whether it was a good thing to have Pompey as a guardian when he was on the run from Julius Caesar was another matter. Pothinus didn't think so. (It meant he was out of a job!) And the people of Alexandria were extremely angry. They hated their kings to be servants of Rome.

WHO SOLD OUR FOOD DOWN THE RIVER?
WHO SENT OUR MEN TO THE WAR?
THE GREEK KING AND QUEEN DID, TO POMPEY,
AND IF HE ASKS THEM, THEY'LL SEND HIM SOME MORE.

WHO JUMPS WHEN ROME WHISTLES?
THE FAT QUEEN
SHE'S NOT STARVING - BUT I AM!

When Pothinus saw how angry the people were, he decided to blame Cleo. It had all been her idea, he said. Young King Ptol had nothing to do with it. The people of Alexandria believed him, and drove Cleopatra out of the city.

Fourth round to Pothinus.

Civil war in Egypt

Cleopatra took refuge in the Egyptian countryside, where the people liked her better. She was out, but not down. She raised an army and it looked as if there would be all-out civil war as Pothinus and the King's army marched against her.

But before the two armies could fight, there came news of a big battle between the Romans. Julius Caesar had beaten Pompey and Pompey had scarpered. He was on his way to Egypt! In September 48 BC, King Ptol's army, camped along the coast waiting to attack Cleopatra, saw Pompey's fleet sail into view.

What to do? Here's the note that Pothinus wrote to himself as he worked out how this would affect him.

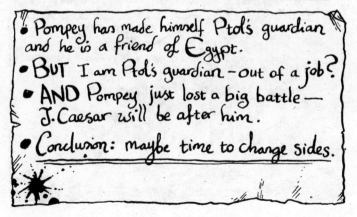

- Pompey has made himself Ptol's guardian and he is a friend of Egypt.
- BUT I am Ptol's guardian – out of a job?
- AND Pompey just lost a big battle – J. Caesar will be after him.
- Conclusion: maybe time to change sides.

Pothinus got together with Ptol's tutor, Theodotus, and the two men hatched a plot. Maybe you can guess what it is if you know that Theodotus said, 'Dead men don't bite.'

They got young King Ptol to dress up in all his royal robes and stand on the beach, ready to greet his guardian.

They sent a small rowing-boat out to Pompey's flagship. In it were an Egyptian general and two Roman soldiers who had served under Gabinius. Pothinus knew Pompey would trust the Romans.

The three in the boat invited Pompey to come ashore – alone. Pompey thought this was a bit odd, but the two Romans said it was just the Egyptian way and he would get a proper welcome on the beach. So Pompey said goodbye to his wife, Cornelia, who was on board ship with him, and climbed down a rope ladder into the small rowing-boat.

Cornelia watched the strip of water widening between the big boat and the little one. Afterwards she wrote to her sister about what happened next.

SISTER,

THE MOST TERRIBLE NEWS, WORSE EVEN THAN THE DEFEAT I WROTE TO YOU ABOUT YESTERDAY. GNAEUS IS DEAD.

HE KNEW THINGS WEREN'T RIGHT WHEN HE STEPPED INTO THE ROWING-BOAT. I SAW HIM CHANGE HIS MIND. REACH FOR THE LADDER AGAIN – BUT IT WAS TOO LATE. ALREADY ACHILLAS WAS ROWING FOR THE SHORE.

THEN, WHEN THEY WERE TOO FAR FROM US TO REACH THEM FOR HELP, BUT NOT YET AT THE SHORE, THERE WAS A SCUFFLE. TWO MEN FELL ON HIM. I HEARD AN AWFUL SCREAM ACROSS THE WATER. THEN SHIPS FROM THE EGYPTIAN NAVY BEGAN TO ATTACK. SOME OF OUR SHIPS WERE SUNK, THE REST FLED AND SCATTERED. I WRITE THIS LETTER FROM CYPRUS WHERE WE PUT IN AFTER TWO DAYS.

I AM SO UNHAPPY I CANNOT THINK STRAIGHT.

YOUR DESOLATE SISTER,

CORNELIA

There were no newspapers in Rome in those days, but if there had been, the story – and what happened next – might have reported something like this:

THE CENTURION
XX/IX/DCCVI (48 BC)

GORY GIFTS FROM GYPS

Caesar's fleet sailed into the great harbour of Alexandria today, two days after the murder of his enemy, Gnaeus Pompey. Caesar had been expecting to fight Pompey. Instead, he was met by Theodotus, tutor to the King of Egypt, who gave him two gory gifts. The first was Pompey's signet ring – badge of a general and proconsul. The second sight made Caesar weep. It was the bloody head of his old colleague.

Caesar's Fury

The King of Egypt thought that Caesar would be pleased with such a ghastly gift – but he was wrong. 'I may have had my differences with Pompey, but you had no business killing him,' said Caesar. 'You seem to have forgotten he was still a Roman leader.'

Theodotus hands Caesar his 'presents'

THE CENTURION
XXVIII/IX/DCCVI (48bc)

ROMANS ON PARADE IN ALEXANDRIA

Caesar marchs through Egypt's capital

Today the citizens of Alexandria watched as Caesar marched at the head of a huge parade through the streets of Alexandria. 'Kings who kill Roman generals can no longer be kings,' said Caesar.

What the Roman papers do not mention is the anger of the Egyptian people. They were furious with Caesar. They thought the parade looked too much like a Roman Triumph – the sort of procession Rome held when a country was conquered. They were not conquered. They still had a king, and this was an insult. Caesar was in for a difficult ride.

67

CAESAR'S JOURNAL

THESE EGYPTIANS ARE A STROPPY LOT. RIOTS AGAIN TODAY. I HAD TO ORDER THE MEN OUT TO RESTORE ORDER.

I DON'T CARE FOR THE EUNUCH. INSOLENT LITTLE RUNT. I'VE BEEN WONDERING WHY ALL OUR MEALS ARE SERVED ON WOODEN PLATES. TODAY I COMMENTED – WHERE'S ALL THE FAMOUS GOLD AND SILVER THE EGYPTIANS ARE SUPPOSED TO EAT OFF? HE HAD THE CHEEK TO TELL ME WE HAD NICKED THE LOT. I ASKED HIM TO EXPLAIN HIMSELF. HE SHRUGGED HIS SHOULDERS, SAID IT HAD ALL BEEN SENT TO ROME TO PAY THE MONEYLENDERS. THE INSOLENCE. I WASN'T HAVING IT. SAID, 'THAT'LL TEACH YOU TO BORROW MONEY THEN, WON'T IT?' IT'S NOT TRUE OF COURSE. HE'S GOT IT STASHED AWAY SOMEWHERE.

TODAY THE OILY LITTLE RUNT HAD THE CHEEK TO TELL ME IT WAS TIME I WENT BACK TO ROME. I TOLD HIM I WAS GOING NOWHERE UNTIL HE MADE UP HIS QUARREL WITH THE YOUNG QUEEN.

THAT DAMN EUNUCH. CENTURIONS IN CHARGE OF SUPPLIES TELL ME THE GRAIN HE SENT WAS MOULDY. HE'S GOING TO PUSH ME TOO FAR ONE OF THESE DAYS.

I WOULDN'T MIND SEEING THE QUEEN. PLAIN LITTLE THING, AS I REMEMBER, BUT WITH A MIND AS SHARP AS A KNIFE. WHENEVER I ASK WHERE SHE IS THE OILY LITTLE RUNT SAYS 'SHE DOESN'T TRUST ME, LORD. SHE WON'T COME NEAR.' CAN'T SAY I BLAME HER.

Cleo was also desperate to get in touch with Caesar. After all, she knew she was in with a chance – her brother and Pothinus were in disgrace for killing Pompey.

CLEOPATRA'S SECRET DIARY

Oh, this is so frustrating! I have to see Caesar! My spies tell me he can't stand Ptolemy and his Fat Friend. Pothinus thinks he can win the people's love by insulting Caesar. He doesn't realize that without Caesar's help, he doesn't stand a chance.

If only I could get to Caesar – but how can I? It's not the Romans I fear, it's my own people. Pothinus

> Would finish me off like Pompey in a flash!
>
> LATER. Have just spoken with my good friend Apollodorus. He has a plan to get me into the palace to meet Caesar. It's dangerous. Very dangerous. If it fails, I've had it. But if I don't get in to see him I've had it anyway. We try tonight.

That night, a small boat sailed into Alexandria. In the bottom of the boat was a long roll of carpet, but the captain did not tie up at the quay which led to the bazaar, where merchants and shopkeepers argued and bargained noisily. Instead he sailed on, his oars lapping quietly in the dark water. He brought his boat in and tied up alongside the palace jetty. Then he got ready to hoist his roll of carpet up on to his shoulder...

70

Cleo had made it into the palace to see Caesar. Now she had to talk fast, before Pothinus heard what she was up to.

How do we know about Cleopatra?

1 Eyewitness accounts
This means someone alive at the time who actually knew her and wrote about her.

Cicero was a member of the senate and a great speaker and writer. He was an old codger who didn't like change when Cleo was a young woman, and he couldn't stand her. He thought she was leading Caesar away from sensible Roman ideas about government towards the dangerous Egyptian idea of god-kings.

I hate the Queen. I cannot speak without pain of her arrogance when she lived in the gardens across the River Tiber.

Then there were other Romans, like the poets **Horace**, **Virgil** and **Propertius**. They were much younger, and it's likely that at first they were dazzled by her. But the writings which have survived come from the time when Cleo had really threatened the Roman Senate. She was The Enemy, and they didn't have a good word to say for her.

Julius Caesar also wrote his own account of events, but he didn't include his love-life, so there is nothing about Cleo.

2 Historians writing after her death
Plutarch was a Greek historian, who wrote a book called *Lives of the Noble Grecians and Romans*. He lived about a hundred years after Cleopatra, but people in his family had known Julius, Antony and Cleo, so he had their letters and journals to work from. His version of Cleo was so vivid that Shakespeare used it for his play *Antony and Cleopatra*.

Josephus was a Jewish historian who wrote a book called *The Jewish Wars*. He was another one who didn't care for Cleo. This was because she diddled Herod, King of the Jews, out of a lot of land.

You can't really blame young Ptolemy for not trusting his big sister. First she had tried to pretend he didn't exist and ruled on her own. Now, just when he thought he had her on the run, she had got the upper hand again. Here's what the steles had to say.

THERE WAS AN OLD ROMAN CALLED CAESAR
A SOLDIER HE WAS, THIS OLD GEEZER
HE COURTED OUR QUEEN
WHO WAS JUST ~~SEVENTEEN~~ Twenty-one more like!
AND NOW HE REFUSES TO LEAVE HER

Yes, when Cleopatra jumped out from the carpet, it was just the beginning for Caesar-and-Cleopatra. All right, so Caesar was bald and old enough to be her dad (he was 52) but he was still a handsome man. Descriptions of him say that he was very tall, with black eyes. He was also interesting, intelligent, strong, brave and – most important of all as far as Cleopatra was concerned – he was the most powerful Roman alive.

As for Caesar, it's not that surprising he found Cleo so attractive. Here's what Plutarch said about her.

> *Her actual beauty was not in itself so remarkable; it was the impact of her spirit that was irresistible. The attraction of her person, joined with the charm of her conversation and the characteristic intelligence of all that she said and did, was bewitching. It was a delight merely to hear the sound of her voice. As if this were an instrument of many strings, she could pass from one language to another, so that in her interviews with barbarians she seldom required an interpreter.*

75

As well as all that, Cleopatra was keen to get on with Caesar – unlike Pothinus. So the battle-weary Caesar and the clever young Queen of Egypt sat and talked. And talked. And talked. And then they fell into each other's arms. Caesar and Cleopatra were in love.

Civil war as usual

When he found out what was going on, kid-brother Ptolemy was hopping mad! What possible influence could he have if Caesar was Cleo's boyfriend? He was so angry he ran out into the streets of Alexandria shouting and screaming. Egged on by Pothinus, Ptolemy tore off his crown, threw it on the ground and jumped on it.

Ptolemy wasn't just throwing a tantrum. He was hoping the Alexandrians would be furious along with him, and rise up against Caesar.

Since the Alexandrians weren't about to fight Caesar, Pothinus ordered the Egyptian army to besiege Alexandria and the palace. Caesar, Cleopatra, Ptolemy and Cleo's younger sister, Arsinoe were all holed up inside. Caesar was keen to keep young Ptol in there with him. That way he could pretend he was just dealing with a little rebellion, not a major civil war.

But he had reckoned without Arsinoe!

Arsinoe versus Cleopatra

Cleo's younger sister had been quietly waiting her chance. This was it. She got a eunuch called Ganymede to help her escape from the palace and take her to the Egyptian army.

Here are her notes for the speech she planned to give to the troops – and to the people of Alexandria.

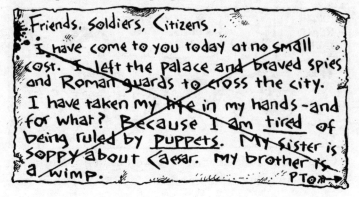

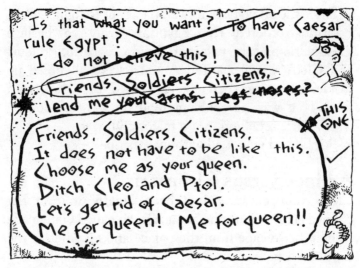

Arsinoe's plot worked – briefly. For a time she found herself leading the Egyptian resistance movement. Unfortunately she didn't get on with the top Egyptian general, Achillas. So she cut off his head and promoted her tutor, the eunuch Ganymede, to take his place.

Ganymede came up with a brilliant idea to make Caesar surrender. He flooded the city's water supply with salt water.

Caesar was a clever man. As well as being a brilliant soldier, he was an explorer and a scientist. He knew how to look at land and see where the most likely place to find water was. He set his soldiers digging, and, sure enough they came to a freshwater spring.

The city was able to survive till Roman reinforcements arrived. And Caesar knew they were on the way.

Meanwhile, back at the palace. . .

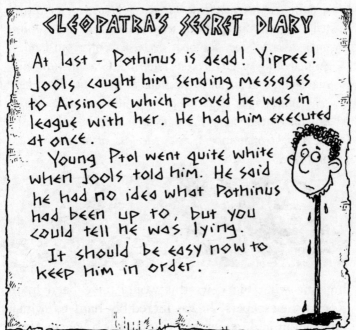

Roman ships to the rescue

In 47 BC, a Roman fleet arrived to lift the siege of Alexandria and rescue Caesar. They quickly took the famous Pharos lighthouse, and Caesar emerged from the palace to try and take control of the Heptastadion, the long strip of land which led out to the lighthouse. That way, the Romans would control the harbour. Unfortunately for Caesar, the Egyptians came in behind the Roman troops and cut them off. Here's what happened next – in Caesar's own words. He wrote the *Alexandrine War* telling all about his battles in Egypt, as if he was talking about someone else. He never used the word 'I'!

> *Caesar, when he saw that they were all giving ground, withdrew to his own boat. He was followed by a crowd who began forcing their way on board, making it impossible to steer the boat or push it off from land. Anticipating what would happen, Caesar jumped overboard and swam to the ships further out. Then he sent small boats to pick up the soldiers in difficulties and thus saved many. As to his own boat, it sank under the weight of numbers, with the loss of all those still on board.*

Imagine what big news this would have been in the Roman newspapers! It was incredibly hard to swim in full armour and, remember, Caesar was 52 at the time.

THE CENTURION
V/III/ DCCVII (47 BC)

GOTCHA!

Months of stalemate ended today when a Roman fleet arrived off Alexandria and took the famous Pharos lighthouse. Signals were sent to Caesar, who has been besieged in the royal palace all winter. Immediately he led his troops out from the palace to take the Hep. But no sooner were our boys out there on the narrow Hep than swarms of Egyptian soldiers attacked from behind, cutting them off from the town.

Caesar Swims to Victory

As the small boat went down, a lone figure could be seen swimming away, a sheaf of papyri held above his head. It was Caesar himself, swimming strongly in helmet and full armour. Every so often he dived underwater to dodge the arrows falling round him. He reached the anchored flagship and within minutes, had ordered every available small boat to rescue the men in the water. By nightfall, Caesar had retaken the Hep and routed the Egyptians. Once again, the old lion had proved he was more of a man than young men half his age. And he even saved his papers! The *Centurion* salutes you, sir!

Caesar: wet but victorious

Ptolemy versus Caesar

Not long after this Caesar told Ptolemy to get lost. Maybe Cleo urged him to. Ptolemy pretended he was really sad to go, but no sooner was he out of the gates than he headed for the Egyptian camp. There he told Arsinoe to get lost and sacked Ganymede as general. He didn't want any big sisters or eunuchs around. He was leader now!

Unfortunately for Ptol, Roman reinforcements were on the way. A big army arrived from Syria, and Caesar's troops met up with them. In the battle that followed, the Romans defeated the Egyptians. Now it was Ptolemy's turn to try and escape by boat. Again, hundreds of panic-stricken soldiers tried to jump on board. Ptolemy wasn't as quick off the mark as Caesar. He drowned, along with everyone else on the boat.

Cleopatra was delighted with Caesar's victory but the average Alexandrian was less happy.

CAESAR MARCHED BACK INTO THE CITY TODAY AT THE HEAD OF THE ROMAN ARMY. THEY LOOKED FIGHTING FIT, THE ROMANS. UNLIKE OUR BOYS, WHO CREPT BACK WOUNDED AND BEATEN. THOSE WHO CAME BACK AT ALL, THAT IS...

HE WAS MET BY THE CITY BOSSES. LAST WEEK THEY WAS ALL ON AT US TO KICK OUT THE ROMAN BULLY. NOW IT WAS YES, CAESAR, NO, CAESAR, THREE BAGS FULL, CAESAR. EVEN PRESENTED HIM WITH THE KEYS OF THE CITY AND THANKED HIM FOR LIBERATING US. MAKES YOU SICK!

THEN SHE APPEARS. THE QUEEN. ALL DONE UP IN HER ROYAL ROBES. GREETS HIM LIKE HE'S RESCUED US. RESCUED *HER* MORE LIKE. 'COS IT SUITS HER JUST FINE TO BE A ROMAN SUBJECT. I DON'T KNOW WHAT'S GOING TO HAPPEN NOW. MY DAD SAYS IT'S THE FIRST TIME IN 300 YEARS THAT ANYONE'S CONQUERED EGYPT.

FIRST THING NEXT MORNING THE ROMANS WERE DREDGING THE RIVER, UP WHERE THE BATTLE WAS. SEEMS THEY KNEW WHAT THEY WERE LOOKING FOR BECAUSE BY LUNCHTIME THEY WERE BACK WITH A BODY IN TOW. THE KING'S BODY.

BY NIGHTFALL THEY HAD HIS ARMOUR ON DISPLAY OUTSIDE THE PALACE. GOLD IT IS. THE SAME ARMOUR HE WAS WEARING WHEN HE LED OUR BOYS INTO BATTLE. SO WE CAN STOP HOPING THE YOUNG KING ESCAPED. HE'S A GONER ALL RIGHT.

Cleo may have thought she was free to rule alone at last, but Caesar had other ideas.

Ptolemy is dead, long live Ptolemy!

CLEOPATRA'S SECRET DIARY

I don't believe it! Jools is saying I have to marry Baby Ptol! He even announced it to the Egyptian people, even though I'd already told them I absolutely do not <u>need</u> another husband, especially not another boy. I tried everything I could to make him change his mind. I told him that *he* was my husband and I didn't need another one. Jools wasn't having it. Reminded me that he was already married and the Romans wouldn't buy it if he ditched his wife. That made me angry. I stamped my foot and said I would never speak to him again, but Jools only laughed and went away, telling me he'd talk to me when I was prepared to be sensible.

BABY PTOL

I sulked for a couple of days but Jools wouldn't budge on baby Ptol. He told me my people expect it. I told him I was queen and they would do as I said. He said, 'They haven't done what you've told them so far.' Which is true, but that was 'cos of horrible old Pothinus.

Jules said this marriage would quieten things down. And get them off his back 'cos they'd see that he respects our customs.

'Won't you be jealous?' I asked him.

'Don't be silly,' said Jools. 'A boy of ten? Everybody knows it's only a pretend marriage.'

'But I want <u>you</u>,' I told him.

He grew very kind and stroked my face. 'I know you do,' he said. Then he explained how he can't be with me very much longer. It's not that he doesn't love me, but he's got a whole empire to rule.

'And what about our library?' I said. Because he adores the library. We spend hours there together, looking at scrolls handwritten by Homer and Plato[1] and talking about everything under the sun. Jools looked sad. He said he would miss it terribly. He said he would miss <u>me</u> terribly.

I couldn't bear the thought of losing him so soon, so I came up with a brilliant idea. I invited him to sail up the Nile with me. I want to show him all the places DF showed me - the real Egypt. At first he said

---

[1]Homer was a Greek poet who wrote the *Iliad* and the *Odyssey*. Plato was a Greek philosopher who wrote the *Republic*.

he couldn't spare the time, but I could see he was taken with the idea, especially when I told him we could take the royal barge and that he needed a rest after all his campaigns. I even promised him I'd marry Baby Ptol if he promised to come away with me.

'You'll marry Baby Ptol whether I come away with you or not,' said Jools. But he didn't say he wouldn't come.

In fact, I know he will. He loves a good time, does Jools. And he doesn't want to leave me, whatever he says.

Cleo did marry Baby Ptol, who became Ptolemy XIV of Egypt. And Caesar and Cleo did go on their river cruise, leaving Arsinoe locked up in the palace.

The spectacular royal barge

LARGE, SUMPTUOUS BEDROOMS.

MUSICIANS.

DINING ROOM.

LOTS OF ACCOMMODATION FOR COURTIERS.

The trip up the Nile was as much summit conference as holiday. And the Nile was the main thoroughfare of Egypt, so it was also a way of showing the Egyptian people that the goddess-queen of Egypt and the strong-man of the Roman Empire were allies.

THE CENTURION

TREATED LIKE ROYALTY

from our Nile Cruise reporter

If Caesar was unpopular when he marched through the streets of Alexandria in Triumph two years ago, all seems forgotten now as he glides up the Nile beside the lively young Queen of Egypt. Caesar is being treated like a king!

It is an amazing sight. The royal barge is like a small conference centre, with oarsmen, cooks, musicians, secretaries, security men and courtiers all rushing about their business day and night. There must be 400 other boats accompanying the royal barge, carrying Roman soldiers and Egyptians. This is the Nile Cruise of all time!

Egypt under water

The mighty Nile is in flood. There is water as far as the eye can see, filling the entire valley between reddish cliffs and mountains. Whole villages are submerged, and the tops of palm trees poke up from the slow-moving waters. As we pass, people line the distant banks to watch the majestic procession and worship their goddess-queen. As we reach the bigger towns, Her Majesty insists the oarsmen take the barge inshore so the people can see her better.

This time of year, when the waters are high, Nile cruises are unusual – but Caesar knows he must soon get back to Rome. And it has its compensations. Last night, when we reached Philae, the waters were so high that we were able to sail right into the great temple of Isis and row by torchlight between the ancient pillars.

Cleopatra looked every inch a goddess-queen, as she stood in the flickering torchlight, dressed in the robes of Isis, in the prow of her royal barge, our proud Roman general, Caesar, at her side.

Homesick soldiers

It is a spectacular sight, but not everyone on this cruise is happy. Caesar seems to have forgotten that his men have wives and children. They have been away from home a long time. They want to go home.

And they do not want their general picking up too many Egyptian ways. Caesar should remember his place is in Rome. He is a great soldier and a citizen of Rome. But he is just that – a citizen. He must not let the enchantress of Egypt fill his head with dreams of being king.

The journalist was right. Caesar's men *were* fed up with him. Though he would have liked to sail with Cleo right to the Ethiopian border, he decided to cut his trip short.

So he said goodbye to Cleo and sailed for Rome. He

took Arsinoe with him. He was going to make an example of her and show what happened to princesses who fought Roman leaders. She would walk in his Triumph. She would also be out of Cleo's way. However, he knew that even with Arsinoe gone, Cleo might have a rebellion on her hands, so he left three Roman legions to take care of her – and to make sure Egypt stayed loyal to Rome.

CLEO AND ROME

ROME

MY DARLING CLEO,

I AM SO PLEASED AT YOUR NEWS. TO THINK I AM GOING TO BECOME A DAD AGAIN[1] AT THE AGE OF 53!!

I NEVER DREAMED, THAT DAY I SAILED INTO ALEXANDRIA, WHAT ADVENTURES LAY IN STORE. I THINK SO OFTEN OF BEING WITH YOU IN THE LIBRARY WITH ALL THOSE WONDERFUL SCROLLS YOU HAVE THERE FROM ALL OVER THE WORLD. AND OF COURSE I THINK OF THE FEASTS AND MUSIC, THE GOLD AND THE PEARLS – SO MANY PEARLS – AND SEEING YOU FOR THE FIRST TIME IN

[1] Caesar had a daughter, Julia, who had been married to Pompey until she died in 54 BC.

THE ROBES OF THE GODDESS ISIS. WHAT A SIGHT YOU WERE IN THAT BLACK CLOAK, AND THAT FANTASTIC RAINBOW-COLOURED DRESS, WITH THE MOON AND SERPENTS IN YOUR GLORIOUS DARK HAIR. . .

BACK HERE IN ROME, IT ALL SEEMS VERY SOMBRE AND DRAB. THERE'S LOTS OF WORK TO BE DONE. TROUBLE IS, WHEN YOU HAVE A SENATE SO MUCH TIME IS SPENT ARGUING ABOUT HOW THINGS SHOULD BE DONE. I THINK WE COULD LEARN A THING OR TWO FROM YOU EGYPTIANS. IN MANY WAYS LIFE WOULD BE SO MUCH EASIER IF WE WEREN'T A REPUBLIC, AND MY PEOPLE THOUGHT OF ME AS A GOD, THE WAY YOUR PEOPLE – OR SOME OF THEM! – THINK OF YOU.

TALKING OF LEARNING FROM EGYPT, I AM BUILDING A NEW LIBRARY HERE AND GATHERING SCROLLS FROM ALL OVER GREECE AND ROME. YOU WILL HAVE TO BE CAREFUL, YOU MAY NOT HAVE THE GREATEST COLLECTION IN THE WORLD FOR MUCH LONGER!

ALSO I HAVE GIVEN ORDERS FOR THE MARSHES AROUND THE TIBER TO BE DRAINED, USING THE SAME SORT OF SYSTEM OF CANALS YOU HAVE AROUND THE NILE. ONCE THAT IT IS DONE, THERE SHOULD BE SOME RICH FARM LAND NEAR THE CITY.

YOU ASK ABOUT ARSINOE. OF COURSE I AM NOT SEEING ANYTHING OF HER. SHE IS A PRISONER HERE, AND ONE I WILL BE GLAD TO SEE EXECUTED

AND OUT OF THE WAY ONCE AND FOR ALL. BESIDES, YOU FORGET – I AM A MARRIED MAN. THE ONLY EGYPTIAN I CARE ABOUT IS YOU.

LOOK AFTER YOURSELF, MY DEAR. HOW FANTASTIC TO THINK THERE WILL SOON BE A LITTLE CHILD UNITING ROME AND EGYPT.

ALL MY LOVE TO YOU,

JOOLS

EAGLE FACT

Triumphs

Roman generals always staged big victory parades when they came back from their campaigns. These were like carnivals, with the soldiers marching through the streets, prisoners walking in chains, and floats carrying gory tableaux of things that had happened on the campaign. When Caesar came back from Egypt he staged four Triumphs, because he'd defeated four lots of enemies.

THE CENTURION
VIII/V/DCCVII (47 BC)

CAESAR'S TRIUMPH

Caesar acknowledges the cheers of the people

Julius Caesar marched in Triumph through the streets of Rome again today – for the fourth time since he returned home last month. This Triumph was to celebrate his victory over the Egyptians.

It was another magnificent spectacle. First came the senators and top generals, then Caesar himself, in purple robes and crown of laurel leaves, riding in a chariot. Behind him came a long line of wagons and floats – and a model of the giant Pharos lighthouse, with a real fire burning at its top.

The tramps of the soldiers' feet and the sound of their voices could be heard long before they came into view. Hundreds of men marched through the city in lines ten abreast. Some mothers in the crowd put their hands over their children's ears so they wouldn't hear the rude words the men were singing about Caesar and the Egyptian Queen.

Princess in chains

Finally came the Egyptian prisoners in chains. They didn't look so cocky now as they did in Egypt. The crowds yelled, 'Kill them, kill them,' as they passed. Right in the middle of them was Princess Arsinoe, walking by herself. She had heavy chains around her ankles and wrists, but she held her head up high.

The crowds fell silent as she passed. Several onlookers said they thought it was wrong to make her walk with the other prisoners. 'She may be an Egyptian and a rebel, but she is a princess,' said Septimia Magna, a married woman.

Another man, who would not give his name, said, 'That Caesar is in Cleopatra's pocket. He does whatever she tells him. She's the one who hates Arsinoe.'

Arsinoe holds her head high

Many of the Egyptian prisoners were killed that day – but not Arsinoe. Maybe Caesar realized it would make him unpopular. Or maybe, just maybe, he wanted another Egyptian up his sleeve, in case Cleopatra got stroppy and wouldn't co-operate with Rome.

ROME

DEAREST CLEOPATRA,

SORRY ABOUT ARSINOE. I KNEW YOU WOULD BE
ANGRY THAT I'D LET HER LIVE. ALL I CAN TELL
YOU IS THAT IT WOULD NOT HAVE GONE DOWN
WELL HERE IN ROME IF I'D HAD HER KILLED. FOR
ALL HER FAULTS SHE HAD A LOT OF DIGNITY, AND
SO I HAVE SENT HER TO LIVE AT A TEMPLE OF
EPHESUS. I WILL MAKE QUITE SURE SHE DOESN'T
TROUBLE YOU – UNLESS OF COURSE, YOU GIVE
ME A HARD TIME!

IT'S ALSO TRUE THAT I HAVE A NEW GIRLFRIEND,
BUT WHAT I AM SUPPOSED TO DO WHEN YOU ARE
SO FAR AWAY? IT DOESN'T MEAN I'VE FORGOTTEN
YOU, FAR FROM IT.

GLAD YOU ARE IN GOOD HEALTH. WILL WRITE
AGAIN SOON.

LOVE,

JOOLS

PS – COULD YOU SEND OVER A COUPLE OF YOUR
ASTROLOGERS? I WANT TO COME UP WITH A NEW
CALENDAR, AND YOUR GUYS ARE MUCH THE BEST.

EAGLE FACT

Roman calendars

Julius Caesar did create a new calendar in 46 BC. It was called the 'Julian calendar' after him. His calendar, like ours, was based on the time the earth takes to go round the sun – the 'solar year'. This is 364 and a quarter days, 11 minutes. Jools – or the astrologers Cleo sent over to help him – rounded this down to 364 and one quarter days (ignoring the 11 minutes) and introduced the idea of a leap year every four years to use up the quarter days. That rounding down was a bit like a clock running fast. Four hundred and seven leap years later – in 1582 AD – ten days had to be dropped from the calendar to get back in step with the sun.

The names of our months also date from Roman times. Jools had 30-day months alternating with 31-day months, except for February which had 28 days (29 in leap years). Naturally, his own month, July, was a big month.

ROME

DEAREST CLEOPATRA,

WHAT GOOD NEWS THAT YOU'VE HAD A HEALTHY BABY BOY! I AM THRILLED. AND YES, I THINK PTOLEMY-CAESAR WOULD BE A GREAT HANDLE FOR HIM. GREAT NEWS FOR THE ROMAN PEOPLE TO THINK THAT ONE DAY THERE WILL BE A 'YOUNG CAESAR' ON THE THRONE OF EGYPT.

WISH I COULD SEE HIM. UNFORTUNATELY I HAVE TOO MUCH TO DO HERE TO GET AWAY. HOWEVER, HOPE TO GET OVER TO EGYPT TO SEE YOU BOTH ONE OF THESE DAYS.

YOUR GOOD FRIEND,

JOOLS

PS YOU SAY I'VE FORGOTTEN YOU. NOT AT ALL, I AM HAVING A LIFE-SIZE STATUE OF YOU MADE IN GOLD, AND DRESSED IN YOUR ROBES OF ISIS. SHE WILL STAND IN THE NEW FORUM, CALLED AFTER ME, BESIDE THE GODDESS VENUS.

A new Ptol in town

Little Ptolemy-Caesar was always known as Caesarion. Maybe Cleo wanted it that way, so that the Romans would never forget that he was Julius Caesar's son. For if Caesar thought in terms of a Roman Caesarion ruling Egypt, Cleo was almost certainly thinking about an Egyptian Ptolemy ruling the Roman Empire.

Every Coin Tells a Story

To make sure she kept in with her Egyptian subjects, Cleo had some new coins minted. On these was a picture of the goddess Isis feeding the god-baby Horus at her breast. Isis – wouldn't you know – looked exactly like the 23-year-old Queen Cleopatra.

To the Egyptians – the real Egyptians rather than the people of Alexandria – this made her more of a goddess-queen. It also made baby Caesarion the god-king.

But it must have given young Ptolemy XIV, Cleo's baby brother-husband, a bit of a scare...

Cleo arrived in Rome that same year, along with her kid-brother husband, her baby son, lots of courtiers, and shiploads of jewels, robes, works of art and manuscripts to give away as presents. Caesar, along with the rest of Rome, was surprised. And his wife Calpurnia was not very pleased.

However, Caesar was the most powerful man in the world. He did what he wanted. And Cleopatra was a visiting queen. He gave her a big villa on his estate by the River Tiber to live in with her court. He often came to visit her there, and so did just about anyone who was anyone in Rome. Even Cicero, the senator who thought she was unbelievably arrogant, went to see her.

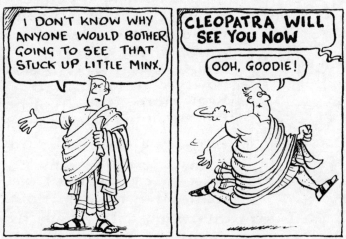

The truth was everyone wanted to meet the exotic Goddess-Queen of Egypt, who dined off plates of gold, and could hold her own with all the best scholars, and spoke nine languages, and gave presents of rare scrolls and jewels to those she liked. Cleopatra was a huge success in Rome.

CLEOPATRA'S SECRET DIARY

Today Jools took me to see the magnificent new forum he has built. It is called after him — the Forum Julium — because it is a shrine to his family. It must have cost an absolute bomb. In it there is a statue of the goddess Venus, who he says is the mother of them all.

Much more interesting is that next to her is a beautiful golden statue — of me !!

I said nothing in public of course. Simply inclined my head graciously and bowed to the goddess Venus. When we were alone however, I wanted to know more. Why had he put me in his family shrine?

Jools grinned and said I knew perfectly well. Obviously, I did, but I wanted him to spell it out.

So I kept on asking, and finally he said it: I'm there 'cos I'm the mother of his child!

My heart gave a little jump when he said this. Does that mean he plans to make our son his heir?

I didn't want to be too forward, so I

> just asked him why there wasn't a statue of Caesarion there too – or come to that, one of Jools himself.
>
> Jools told me not to be silly. He said it was more than his life was worth to put a statue of himself in his own forum. He said the Roman Senate wouldn't stand for it. They would think he was saying he was a god.
>
> I told him he was a god to me. He liked that. I think he still loves me. It's just politics that makes him keep his distance here in Rome. I'm so glad I have no Senate I have to watch out for. And he wishes he had no Senate too. He's told me as much. Maybe one day he'll find a way to declare himself king.

Cleopatra wasn't the only one who knew Julius Caesar was fed up with the republic. Many of his fellow senators knew it too. Some of them were pleased. They agreed with Caesar that Rome needed one strong ruler to keep the vast empire in order.

Others loathed the idea. They thought J. Caesar had become very arrogant and they blamed Cleopatra for leading him astray. They hated the way he had brought so many Egyptian ideas back to Rome.

Caesar's sticky end

In the spring of 44 BC, JC was just about to go off to war again. He was going to fight the King of Parthia. If he conquered Parthia it would mean he ruled as much of the world as Alexander the Great had. Knowing he would be gone for a long time, Cleopatra decided to go home.

But JC never conquered Parthia. Two days before he was due to leave, he was stabbed to death by some of his fellow senators as he made his way to the Senate. Julius Caesar was dead.

CLEOPATRA'S SECRET DIARY

He's gone. My protector. My friend.

I thought he might die in Parthia, in battle, but to die like this — murdered by his own people! How could they? They will never have a leader like him again—so brave, so strong, so brilliant.

I'm not the widow, and yet I miss him. I miss him terribly.

And what about our son? What's going to happen to him now? I should go home, but I think I'll stay just in case. The will is read next week. Maybe, just maybe, Jools has named him his heir.

Cleopatra hung on in Rome, even though she knew there were things she should be doing back in Egypt. Then the fateful day came.

CLEOPATRA'S SECRET DIARY

The will was read today. I still cannot believe it. No mention of Caesarion. Jools has left him exactly nothing. Instead his great-nephew, Octavius, is to get most of his land and money.

Why? He can't have been afraid of what people would think. He had already made it clear Caesarion was his son. Why else did he put my statue in the Forum Julium?

As for Octavius, he's a cold fish. Eighteen and very uptight. I don't think I'll ever make a conquest out of him.

There is nothing here in Rome for me now. I must get back to Egypt. I have neglected Egypt for too long.

Cleopatra was right. Her hope of being queen-mother in Rome was gone. Not only that, her protector was dead and Octavius didn't seem too impressed with her. She was right to go home. The big question was, would she be able to hold on to her throne without Julius Caesar?

HOME ALONE

THINGS TO DO

Check market prices of dates, figs, olives, corn.

FAMINE EMERGENCY – decide who gets grain.

READ RIOT ACT ABOUT CITY LABOURERS – why should they pay extra tax?

HAIRDRESSER   Build tomb[1]

PTOLEMY??? – Reach a decision?

See designer about new coins

Order new sculptures for temple at Denderah.

Write books.

Strengthen borders — HOW???

Find new tutor for Caesarion

---

[1] It was quite usual for Egyptian rulers to start building their tombs while they were still young and healthy.

When Cleopatra came home from Egypt, she was a working mum, and a busy one at that.

While she was away, there had been two years when the Nile did not rise high enough to feed the people. That meant two years of famine. Cleo's governors in the provinces had done what they could, but they couldn't magic crops out of thin air.

It wasn't possible to feed everyone, so Cleo had to decide how much food the country should send to the town – and who should get it. She knew that the farmers had to have enough to survive, because without them, the whole country would starve. She made some tough decisions and made herself unpopular with the people she put at the bottom of the list.

Then after famine came disease. People were weak from lack of food. They died like flies.

Four down, one to go

Someone else died around that time. No one knows how, or why, but rumour was that he'd been poisoned.

Young Ptolemy, coming up to fourteen and starting to get stroppy about his rights, took ill and died not long after he returned to Egypt. Now, out of Cleo's five brothers and sisters, only Arsinoe was still alive.

Baby Ptol's death suited Cleo very nicely because. . .

1 She could make her baby son, Caesarion, her co-ruler. She hoped that this would mean Rome would leave Egypt alone, knowing there was a tiny Roman on the throne.

2 Caesarion was only three so she wouldn't have to consult him about anything for a long time yet.

Cleopatra and Son, Ltd

To celebrate the fact that it was now Cleopatra and Son who ruled Egypt, Cleo had huge figures carved in sandstone at the temple at Denderah. One was herself, a.k.a. the goddess Isis; the other was a grown-up Caesarion.

It was a message to the people of upper Egypt that their queen and king were mother and son – just as it should be.

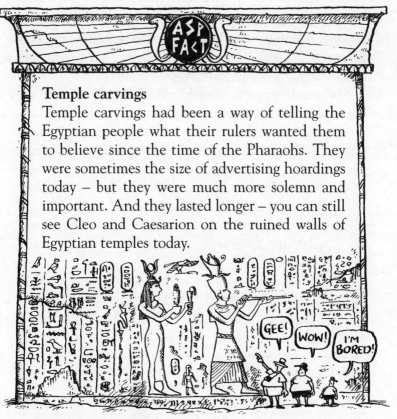

Temple carvings
Temple carvings had been a way of telling the Egyptian people what their rulers wanted them to believe since the time of the Pharaohs. They were sometimes the size of advertising hoardings today – but they were much more solemn and important. And they lasted longer – you can still see Cleo and Caesarion on the ruined walls of Egyptian temples today.

Cleopatra worked hard ruling her country. She was a good business-woman. She was still paying off her father's debts to Rome. Nevertheless, for the first time in generations, money was also coming into the coffers of Egypt.

If there had been an internet in those days, Cleo would have been watching share prices like a hawk. She took an interest in the prices that farmers could get for their crops. She made trade agreements with neighbouring rulers and set up a safe trade route between

111

the Red Sea and the Mediterranean. She developed the porphyry quarries which extracted this beautiful pink and red stone, made from volcanic lava, so it could be polished and used in decorative building.

She also listened to her advisers. She made some good laws, and saw they were carried out fairly.

Because of all these things, Cleopatra became more popular. The farming people, the real Egyptians, had always had a soft spot for her, ever since the day she rowed the bull to the temple. Gradually, as she turned the economy round, the Alexandrians began to think she wasn't so bad after all. She was dead glamorous and she had her head screwed on tight. They began to like their queen.

Civil war in Rome, continued...

Julius Caesar had been murdered by plotters, so it wasn't surprising that civil war broke out again after his death.

ON ONE SIDE - OCTAVIUS CAESAR, HELPED BY MARK ANTONY

ON THE OTHER SIDE - BRUTUS AND CASSIUS, TWO OF THE MEN WHO MURDERED JULIUS

Cleopatra had known Mark Antony from the time she was a teenage girl. He had come to Egypt with Gabinius to put her father back on the throne. She had met him loads of times when she was living in Rome. He was a huge, handsome man, but Cleopatra had never taken a lot of notice of him. Maybe this was because he wasn't interested in the things she was – books, learning, science; he liked drinking and having lots of girlfriends instead. Or maybe he just wasn't powerful enough for her to need to bother with him then.

That was about to change. Just over a year after Caesar had been killed, Cleo received a letter.

TO HER MAJESTY, QUEEN CLEOPATRA OF EGYPT,

AS YOU KNOW, CASSIUS, MURDERER OF JULIUS CAESAR, HAS CONQUERED MOST OF ASIA MINOR. WE ARE ABOUT TO FINISH HIM OFF ONCE AND FOR ALL. PLEASE SEND AS MANY WARSHIPS AS YOU CAN TO HELP US SEE HIM OFF.

YOURS,

OCTAVIAN[1] AND ANTONY

[1] Octavius called himself Octavian once he became a Triumvir.

CLEOPATRA'S SECRET DIARY

How dare they? Who do they think they are, demanding Egyptian warships? Don't they know I've got famine and plague here? How are we supposed to send a navy at a time like this? This is Rome's struggle, not ours.

Besides, what happens if Cassius wins? We'll have had it if we've supported the other side.

There's no way I am going to send warships. They can whistle for them. But I'd better not say that, just in case they win.

So what shall I say?

Probably best to say nothing. Just not answer...

Cleo wasn't able to keep out of the fight for long. Soon she got a message from her spy in Ephesus who kept an eye on her sister.

Dear Majesty,

Thought you should know a. s. a. p. that Arsinoe has declared herself Queen of Egypt again. Seems that she is in touch with Cassius and he's said he will back her claim to the throne in return for her support.

Sorry to be the bearer of bad tidings. Please don't execute me.

Your faithful, most loyal servant,
MARDIAN

CLEOPATRA'S SECRET DIARY

That does it! If Cassius is backing Arsinoe, then I'm against him. Have ordered a fleet to be prepared immediately to go and fight alongside Antony and Octavian. Will sail myself in the flagship at the head of the fleet. I don't want those Romans grabbing my ships. I don't trust any of them. Next thing I know they'll be using them against me to put my manky sister on the throne.

I knew Arsinoe should never have been allowed to live. I told Jools

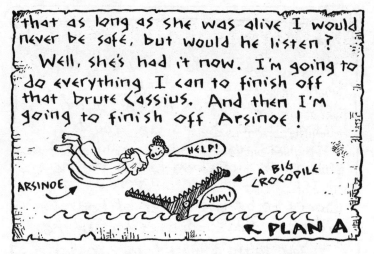

Cleopatra wasn't the sort of queen to stay at home and send an admiral. She put to sea herself at the head of her fleet to fight Cassius. It wasn't her most successful appearance.

TALE OF AN EGYPTIAN SAILOR

What a night it was. I never knew a storm like it. I was aboard the Caesarion along with the Queen, and I thought none of us would see the light of day.

We sailed out of Alexandria on the evening tide. Wind was getting up, but you expect that. Queen had come aboard just afore we cast off. What a sight she was – she was in her royal robes, but with a man's breastplate on her. Nodded to us all as she came on board. We were all standing waiting on her, a guard of honour you might say. She's something else, I tell you. Like she's got a light shining out of her, she is. Those dark eyes, when they look at you, you feel you're getting some of the royalty, somehow. Not that she's beautiful, exactly, but you can't take your eyes off her, just the same.

She went below decks, her and her servants. But when we put out from port she was up on deck, right in the prow of the ship. Like she was our figurehead or something. She stood there a long while, spray blowing in her face.

117

The wind was behind us at this stage, see. Sails were full. She was joking with some of the men – she speaks our language like a native, you might say. You'd never know she was Greek. She said we'd be across the sea and fighting the evil Cassius, who was threatening the security of Egypt, by morning. But I dunno. Somehow I got a bad feeling, I could feel the wind getting up too fast somehow, big gusts, and the boat was pitching and tossing. I remember thinking, 'If we don't drown, Ma'am.' Not that you'd say that to her, of course. Least, I wouldn't.

Next thing I saw, she was hanging over the rails, puking her guts out. And her ladies. They didn't look too regal then, I can tell you.

We can't have been out from Alexandria more than about two hours, when the wind swung round. We didn't even have time to furl the sails, they was ripped from the rigging as we lowered them. The seas crashed right over the boat, it was pitching at an angle of

BLECCCH!

nearly 80 degrees. My mate fell and broke his arm. Two other men were washed overboard. Queen had gone below by now. Passed me as she went down below. Green she was, lurching as the ship pitched.

Behind us the other ships were all trying to steer for cover. No formation left, we was blown all over the place. Couldn't tell which was which in the rain and the dark, but I saw one of the smaller vessels had split clean in two. Men in the water, but we couldn't stop to pick 'em up, we couldn't stop. We was being blown back into the shore, the oarsmen couldn't hardly slow us down. I could see the fire atop the Pharos lighthouse, but what to do? In the end, by some miracle, Queen's luck maybe, we scudded back into the harbour. But some of the other ships ran aground along the coast. Some never made it.

'You did well to bring us back safely,' Queen said to the skipper, as she went ashore. Still white as a sheet she was. You could see she didn't think she was going to last the night. Nor any of us.

119

In the end, Mark Antony and Octavian finished off Cassius without any help from Cleopatra. MA and Octavian didn't like each other much, so they decided to keep out of each other's way. Octavian would rule the western half of the empire and Antony the eastern part.

When Cleopatra heard this, she was quite relieved. It meant she had to deal with Antony. She thought Antony might be friendlier towards her than Octavian, who wasn't very happy that she was the mother of his uncle's only son. But Antony wasn't feeling very friendly towards Cleo. He was annoyed that she hadn't sent warships to his aid when he needed them. (He didn't know her fleet had been wrecked in the storm.) He decided it was time he sent for her and showed her who was boss.

ANTONY AND CLEOPATRA

The barge she sat in, like a burnish'd throne,
Burn'd on the water. The poop was beaten gold;
Purple the sails, and so perfumed that
The winds were love-sick with them; the oars were silver,
Which to the tune of flutes kept stroke, and made
The water which they beat to follow faster,
As amorous of their strokes. For her own person,
It beggar'd all description. She did lie
In her pavilion, cloth-of-gold, of tissue. . .

That is the way Shakespeare described Cleopatra's arrival in Tarsus in his play *Antony and Cleopatra*. He got everything in this speech from Plutarch, who got it from eyewitness accounts: the boat with the golden bow, the purple sails, and Cleopatra herself, reclining on cushions beneath an awning made of golden cloth.

Cleo had kept Antony waiting for several months. (Maybe she was working with her dress and set designers!) She certainly didn't come running to Tarsus the first time he summoned her. And when she did arrive, people could smell her before they saw her, because the flower petals were knee-deep in the cabins.

Everyone rushed to the river banks to see this vision – everyone except poor old Antony, who was left sitting in lonely splendour in the town market-place, waiting for Cleo to come and kneel before him.

Eventually he realized there was nothing for it. He would have to go to meet her.

When he got to the river bank he was as amazed as everyone else. Instead of sailors manning the sails, her waiting women held the ropes, dressed as goddesses and mermaids, while little boys dressed as cupids surrounded Cleopatra. Cleo looked *sensational*.

On top it all Antony and Cleo were meeting in the city of Tarsus, on the river Cydnus. Tarsus had been known for centuries as the place where the goddess of love, Aphrodite, met the god Dionysus. Cleo was dressed as Aphrodite (HINT HINT). The role of Dionysus had still to be filled. Antony rather fancied himself for the part. (He liked a drink.)

123

Here's what Plutarch tells us happened next:

> *Antony invited Cleopatra to dine with him, but she thought it more fitting that he should come to her; so most courteously, he accepted and went. He found the preparations made for him magnificent beyond words. But what astonished him most was the infinite number of lights and torches, as artfully arranged in devices and patterns, some round and some square, that their brilliance amazed the eye and took the breath away. Next day, Antony feasted her, intending to surpass her in magnificence and elegance, but he was hopelessly outdone in both so that he, with his equal good spirits, was the first to pour scorn on his own meagre entertainment. Then Cleopatra saw that he had a soldierly humour, broad and coarse, and she began to pay him in his own coin, teasing him thoroughly and without fear.*

In other words, big, bold, brave, generous Antony fell right under Cleopatra's spell.

The Romans were livid. They said it proved she was a loose woman. But Cleopatra didn't have a steamy love-life. She only had two boyfriends in her entire life. It was just that both of them were VPRs (Very Powerful Romans) and she wasn't married to them.

VPRs were necessary to Cleopatra because she had to keep Rome sweet so Egypt could remain a free country. If Antony had still been a general under Gabinius, Cleo probably wouldn't have given him a second look.

As it was, Ant 'n' Cleo went on to have one of the most famous love affairs of all time.

True love?

However calculating Cleopatra was at the start – and it does look as if she set out to make Antony fall in love with her – by the end they both seem to have really loved one another.

However, Antony 'n' Cleopatra were more than lovers. They were also heads of state making a political alliance. The proof is that they did some hard bargaining in those first heady days when they got together.

125

So Cleo took Antony back home with her, and Arsinoe got the chop. Ant and Cleo had a wild time. They threw parties for each other every night, competing as to who could put on the most lavish supper. Or they would go out on the town. Antony liked to dress up as a slave and go and peer into people's houses. Cleopatra went with him dressed as a servant girl. Antony was often drunk and got into fights, but the Alexandrians liked him for it – and their queen for having the nerve to go with him on his adventures.

Back in Rome, wild stories were told of the new couple. Here's some of the tales, but do you think they're true or false?

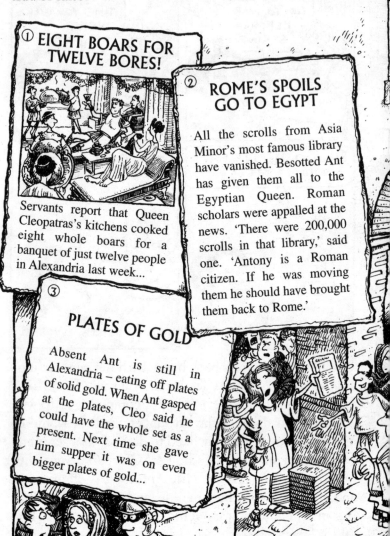

① **EIGHT BOARS FOR TWELVE BORES!**

Servants report that Queen Cleopatras's kitchens cooked eight whole boars for a banquet of just twelve people in Alexandria last week...

② **ROME'S SPOILS GO TO EGYPT**

All the scrolls from Asia Minor's most famous library have vanished. Besotted Ant has given them all to the Egyptian Queen. Roman scholars were appalled at the news. 'There were 200,000 scrolls in that library,' said one. 'Antony is a Roman citizen. If he was moving them he should have brought them back to Rome.'

③ **PLATES OF GOLD**

Absent Ant is still in Alexandria – eating off plates of solid gold. When Ant gasped at the plates, Cleo said he could have the whole set as a present. Next time she gave him supper it was on even bigger plates of gold...

④ QUEEN DRINKS PEARL

Spendthrift Cleopatra's extravagance reached a new height last night when the Queen of Egypt *drank a pearl!*

It seems Ant had been so impressed at what the shopaholic Queen spends on banquets that he asked how she did it. Cleo said this was nothing, and named the figure she would spend next time. 'Impossible,' said Antony.

But next time she threw a party, Cleo called for a pearl. She dropped it into a glass of wine. Then, when the pearl had dissolved, she drank the wine. . .

⑤ LOVER BOY ANT IGNORES KINGS TO READ LOVE STONES

Roman Antony was sitting in judgement on kings and princes yesterday – when he broke off to read a love letter from Cleopatra. As lawyers argued, Ant broke off proceedings – because a messenger had arrived from Cleo. He gave Ant a note from her – scratched on a piece of priceless crystal.

Answers:

1 Apparently true. They cooked them at slightly different times so that however long the Queen delayed the meal, there would always be one boar roasted to perfection. No mention of what happened to the boars they didn't eat, but probably the cooks took home BIG doggy bags.

2 True. Antony did give Cleopatra the entire contents of the library at Pergamum. He wasn't that keen on reading himself, but he knew she adored books.

3 Could be true. Part of Cleopatra's appeal was that she was fabulously wealthy and generous – when she wanted to be.

4 Definitely false. Pearls don't dissolve in wine, and anything they do dissolve in you couldn't possibly drink. However, Cleo may have played a trick on Antony – she may have swallowed the pearl and waited for it to come out the other end! But people believed it at the time – and the fact the Queen 'drank pearls' made her seem more exotic than ever.

5 Maybe partly true. It's quite likely Antony found Cleo's love-letter more interesting than some boring old court case. It seems less likely she would have scratched a love-letter on a piece of crystal – it would have taken so long to write it.

The Romans liked to think Antony was a good Roman boy who was being led astray by the wicked, pleasure-loving Egyptian Queen, but Plutarch tells a story which suggests it wasn't quite like that.

One day when Cleo and Antony were out on the river – yet another day of sun, sea, sand and fishing – she told one of her servants to tie a dead, salted fish to

Antony's fishing line while Antony wasn't looking. The servant then gave the line a tug, and Antony, thinking he had a catch, pulled in the dead fish. Everyone roared with laughter at the joke, including Cleo and Antony. But it's what Cleo said which is interesting.

> *General, you had better give up your rod. Your sport is to hunt cities and kingdoms and continents.*

In other words, 'Enough playing around, Ant. It's time you got on with your career.'

The end of the affair?

Antony and Cleopatra seem to have been very happy together at this stage in their lives. However there was one little problem. Antony was married.

His wife was a very bossy woman called Fulvia. Antony didn't like her much, and didn't want to go home to her. But then came news from Rome. Fulvia had started a civil war against Octavian, Antony's co-ruler. Antony had to leave to sort it out. By the time he got back, Octavian had defeated Fulvia and driven her out of Italy. She died not long afterwards in Greece. This meant Antony was free to marry.

Now it happened that the husband of Octavian's sister had just died. So Octavian had a plan which he thought would turn Antony into an ally – and get rid of the evil Egyptian Queen at the same time. Why didn't Antony marry his sister?

'Great idea,' said Antony, not wanting to offend Octavian. Besides, he had always known he could never marry Cleo, because Romans were only allowed to marry Romans. All the same, he knew Cleo wouldn't be very pleased – especially because when he left she was expecting his baby.

DEAREST CLEO,

BY THE TIME YOU RECEIVE THIS, I WILL BE MARRIED. PLEASE DON'T BE ANGRY. I HAD TO MARRY TO KEEP THE PEACE WITH OCTAVIAN. AFTER THE MESS FULVIA MADE OF THINGS, I HAD TO MADE A BIG GESTURE SO HE WOULD TRUST ME. HE WOULD HAVE BEEN INSULTED IF I HAD TURNED DOWN HIS SISTER. AND I COULD NEVER MARRY YOU, BECAUSE YOU'RE NOT A ROMAN.

OF COURSE I DON'T FEEL ABOUT HER THE WAY I FEEL ABOUT YOU. MY MONTHS WITH YOU HAVE BEEN THE MOST EXCITING OF MY WHOLE LIFE. I SHALL MISS YOU MORE THAN YOU WILL EVER KNOW. I HOPE ONE DAY WE WILL BE VERY SPECIAL FRIENDS.

ALL MY LOVE, DARLING,

ANTONY

Needless to say, Cleo was livid. Who wouldn't be? Antony had been her boyfriend for more than a year. She was expecting his baby. And probably most important of all to Cleopatra, she needed him for her master plan: she wanted Rome and Egypt to be allied through the marriage of their rulers.

CLEOPATRA'S SECRET DIARY

How dare he! How DARE he?!!?! Marry Octavian's sister when he could have come back and married me! I can't believe it! He said he loved me. I KNOW he loves me. Yet he casts me off in order to marry some boring Roman widow, just to keep Octavian sweet.

And they are going to live in Athens. How can he do this? How can he pretend the last year never happened? He can't. Our child is evidence. He'll want to see the baby once it's born.

I never loved him anyway. Big boring carthorse of a man. No brains. Crass. Drunk half the time. No interest in anything remotely intellectual. I'm better off without him.

I am going to send a spy to his court. An astrologer. I know how superstitious Ant is.

Letters from Egypt – sent and unsent

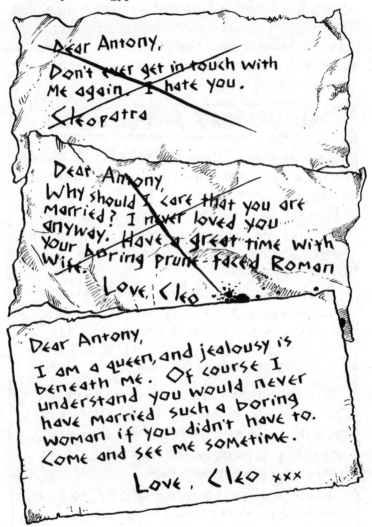

Dear Antony,
Don't ever get in touch with me again. I hate you.
Cleopatra

Dear Antony,
Why should I care that you are married? I never loved you anyway. Have a great time with your boring prune-faced Roman wife.
Love, Cleo

Dear Antony,
I am a queen, and jealousy is beneath me. Of course I understand you would never have married such a boring woman if you didn't have to. Come and see me sometime.
Love, Cleo xxx

Cleo never did things by halves. In 40 BC she gave birth to twins – Antony's children. She called them

Cleopatra (who'd have thought?) and Alexander (there already was a Ptolemy – young Caesarion, her son by Julius Caesar).

It would be three years before she saw Antony again. He was living in Athens with Octavian's sister, who was called Octavia. Cleopatra sent an astrologer to live at his court to spy on them and tell her what was going on. The astrologer wrote to her every day, so she was always bang up to date.

However hurt and angry she was, Cleopatra didn't spend her whole life pining. She still had a country to run. And she had loads of interests. She read a lot. She studied science. Some of the time she may even have looked after the children.

Here are some of the projects she completed:

• a book on make-up
• a book on gynaecology (women's medicine)
• a book on weights and measures
• the design and building of a huge monument which she planned to be her own tomb

This is not a made-up recipe but do NOT try it on your dad – or anyone else! The Greek doctor, Galen, copied it from Cleopatra's book on make-up which has since been lost. We don't know what else Cleo wrote in her book. Was she telling us all about henna and kohl and how to make long wigs, like the ancient Egyptians? Or was she into drinking lots of water, and taking exercise? There is a legend that she used to bathe in asses' milk – presumably because it was good for the skin.

In addition to all this Cleo was famous for studying the secrets of the Ancient Egyptians. Some of these secrets were supposed to give you special, superhuman powers.

This was all part of being a goddess-queen. And that's what mattered to Cleopatra most of all, far more than the loss of Antony. She was Queen of Egypt, and she meant to stay that way, with him or without him. From what she heard, he was getting pretty fed up with Octavia.

Letter from an astrologer

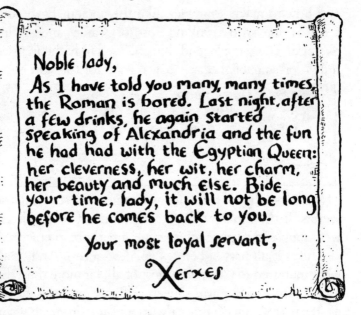

Noble lady,
As I have told you many, many times,
the Roman is bored. Last night, after
a few drinks, he again started
speaking of Alexandria and the fun
he had had with the Egyptian Queen:
her cleverness, her wit, her charm,
her beauty and much else. Bide
your time, lady, it will not be long
before he comes back to you.

Your most loyal servant,

Xerxes

Meet me in Antioch?

The astrologer was right. Antony had had enough of the good but boring Octavia. He left his marriage in the spring of 37 BC. He took off for Antioch and sent a message to Cleo asking her to join him. She came, bringing with her the twins, now three years old, whom Antony had never seen.

Antony was thrilled to see them all. But Cleopatra wasn't the sort of woman to say 'All is forgiven' just like that. If Antony wanted her back, he had to prove he loved her.

She didn't want flowers and sweetmeats either. The way to Cleopatra's heart was always by helping her country. She wanted Antony to strengthen Egypt. That meant giving her land at the edge of Egypt which would make her borders more secure. Or land which was rich in gold or crops. Or preferably both.

Here's what the Jewish historian Josephus wrote about her in the first century AD.

> *At this time there were revolutions and troubles in Syria; for Cleopatra constantly poisoned Antony's mind against the local rulers. She persuaded him to remove them from government, and give their lands and titles to herself. And Antony loved her extremely. He thought the world of her.*
>
> *In this way, she begged Antony to give her the kingdom of Judaea, and to expel the kings of Arabia from their lands. He was so bewitched by this woman that he obeyed her in whatever she asked of him.*

You can tell Josephus didn't much like Cleo! He wasn't the only one. Antony expelled the rulers of Phoenicia and Chalcis in order to give their kingdoms to Cleopatra. He also gave her the Red Sea coast where Arabs called Nabataeans lived, and the part of the Jewish kingdom of Judaea where valuable palm trees grew.

This made a lot of enemies. And it disgusted Antony's fellow Romans – not because Antony was getting rid of kings and grabbing their countries (Rome was always doing that) but because he was giving those countries to the Queen of Egypt.

He wasn't giving them for nothing, though. In exchange Cleopatra agreed to build a fleet of ships. The Egyptian navy would guard the Mediterranean Sea for Antony. And as well as that, Cleo would keep his army supplied with food and clothing.

They held a big ceremony, a bit like a marriage or a coronation to celebrate their deal. Of course, Antony was not free to marry under Roman law, but by this time he was fed up with the Roman way of doing things. He was dreaming dreams like Cleopatra.

I WILL BE A SECOND ALEXANDER THE GREAT! I WILL RULE OVER AS MUCH OF THE WORLD AS HE DID. ALL RIGHT, SOME OF IT BELONGS TO CLEO, BUT SHE'S MY WOMAN, SO THAT MAKES IT MINE.

I WILL BE THE GREATEST QUEEN OF EGYPT THE WORLD HAS EVER KNOWN, GREATER EVEN THAN MY GREAT-GREAT-GREAT-AUNT ARSINOE II. SO WHAT IF I CAN'T DO IT WITHOUT ANT'S HELP– I CAN WRAP HIM ROUND MY LITTLE FINGER.

We can never be sure who really was the boss. By this time they were operating as a team. That year they issued some more new coins, with Antony's head on one side and Cleo's on the other.

They also began dating time again – from the year when they got back together! (The last Big Event in Egyptian history was when young Caesarion began ruling with his mother.) It was a clear message to the world that A&C were an item.

Finally, the twins were given posh new names. Helios, the Greek word for the sun, was added to Little Alexander's name. And Little Cleopatra was called Selene, after the moon. This was one in the eye for Rome's old enemy, the King of Parthia, who called himself the Brother of the Sun and Moon. Antony was telling him to look out! The Romans were coming.

ANTONY GOES TO WAR

The Roman Empire – even just half of it – was so big that no single person could control it directly, so Antony, like other Romans before him, ran a sort of protection racket. The local king could rule, provided he didn't cause any trouble, and gave Antony what he wanted. King Herod of Judaea (the same King Herod who was on the throne when Jesus was born) and Cleopatra were both 'client' rulers like this. They paid their protection money.

The King of Parthia, on the other hand, didn't want to be part of the Roman Empire. He wasn't going to send men and gold to help Rome fight her wars. He wanted to rule his own kingdom.

Antony couldn't allow this to go on. Besides, there was another good reason to conquer Parthia. If he won, it would mean he ruled over as much land as Alexander the Great, the most famous general in all history, and the man with whom Cleo's ancestor, the first Ptolemy, had come to Egypt. Antony liked the idea of that.

So all through the winter of 37 BC, or '1 A&C',

Antony was sending out letters to all his client kings. He filled in different numbers for different kings, according to what he thought they could afford.

MOST DEAR AND SPECIAL ————,

GREETINGS TO YOU FROM ALEXANDRIA.

WHAT A GREAT JOB YOU ARE DOING RULING YOUR BIT OF THE ROMAN EMPIRE. WE ARE VERY GRATEFUL FOR THE CONTRIBUTION YOU MAKE TO THE GLORY OF ROME.

THE ROMAN EMPIRE WILL SOON BE EVEN MORE GLORIOUS. PLEASE SEND THE FOLLOWING:

___ HUNDRED MEN, FULLY ARMED

___ THOUSAND MEN TO SERVE AS PORTERS, COOKS, MEDICS ETC.

___ TONNES OF GRAIN

___ HUNDRED MULES

___ CAMELS

___ BRIDLES

___ SADDLES

___ PANNIERS

___ PAIRS OF LEATHER SANDALS (VARIOUS SIZES)

___ BANDAGES

YOURS,

ANTONY
TRIUMVIR OF ROME

In addition, he sent out a summons to all the Roman legions in his territories. They were to assemble in Antioch, ready for war. These men were all seasoned soldiers.

And when the winter was over, Antony set off from Antioch for Parthia at the head of an enormous army – and Cleo went with him part of the way.

CLEOPATRA'S SECRET DIARY

DAY ONE

How handsome Ant looks marching at the head of his Roman army in his leather tunic and Roman helmet. He is so strong. I just love his legs in those metal shin protectors. And his men absolutely adore him, that's obvious. He speaks to them as equals, he remembers their names and something about each of them. He's always got a good word for everyone. I feel quite jealous of them. They're going to have him with them all through the next summer, and I'm not.

DAY FOUR

They march so far, so fast, these Romans. They cover thirty miles a day. I am carried in a litter by four soldiers, otherwise I wouldn't be able to keep up. And all along the route people watch us pass. It is very good for them all to see me there too. It brings home to them that Ant and I are a team.

The Romans are saying that Ant is going to war too early in the year. That he does it to get back home to me before the winter. Ant says that's rubbish, he's marching now because it's cooler.

I have been sick these past three mornings. I think I must be pregnant again.

BLEEURGH

The Romans soldiers weren't very pleased that Cleo was travelling with them. They thought women should stay at home and leave the fighting to the men. But Cleo wasn't going all the way. She had other fish to fry.

DAY TEN

Two days ago we reached the river Euphrates, and camped on its banks. Yesterday and today I watched the men, thousand upon thousand of them, crossing the river in a fleet of small boats which Ant had commandeered from the local fishermen. The boats rowed back and forth, back and forth, ferrying them all. Then the pack animals swam across. Their panniers were taken by boat to keep them dry.

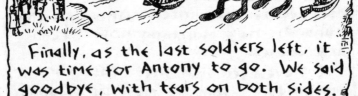

Finally, as the last soldiers left, it was time for Antony to go. We said goodbye, with tears on both sides.

I pray to Ra and the goddess Isis that he conquers Parthia and comes back safe to me in Alexandria.

And now I must attend to my own business.

A nice little earner

Thanks to all the land Antony had given her, the River Euphrates was now the border of Egypt. After Cleo had waved goodbye to Ant, she came back slowly through her new kingdoms. She wanted the people there to see their new queen. And she wanted to talk to their rulers.

I THINK THAT SHOULD BE 'EX RULERS'...

MUTTER GRUMBLE SNARL

This is what Josephus, the Jewish historian said about her visit to King Herod:

> When Cleopatra had settled her affairs and seen Antony as far as the Euphrates River, she came back again and took in Apamea and Damascus on her way to Judaea, where she was honourably received by Herod, who signed a treaty with her that he would send her the revenue of that part of Arabia and Jericho which had been granted to her. The latter being a place famous for balsam which is the most precious of all gums and likewise for the fairest palm trees in the world.

In other words, Cleo did a deal with Herod. His people were allowed to go on farming the balsam groves – which had previously belonged to him – provided he paid Cleopatra for the privilege. No wonder Cleo was rich. And no wonder the Jews disliked her.

Josephus goes on: *'On this occasion she set all her wits to engage Herod in a love affair, and being a woman naturally lustful and shameless, she did as good as meet him halfway.'*

Did Cleo make a pass at Herod? It doesn't seem very likely. It didn't fit with her grand plan, to rule the world with Antony. However, she may have been trying to trap Herod into making a pass at her. If she had succeeded, she could have told Antony, who would have been very angry – and maybe given her even more of King Herod's lands. Josephus reckoned she was plotting to have King Herod put to death.

And another nice little earner

Like King Herod, King Malchus of Nabataea had lost a lot of land when Antony gave it to Cleopatra. It was valuable because it bordered on the Red Sea and beneath it lay a lot of bitumen. Cleopatra made the same sort of trade deal with Malchus as she had made with Herod. She leased the lands by the Red Sea back to him. He could have the bitumen, provided he paid her for it. It was a bit like someone stealing your house, and then charging you rent to live in it.

148

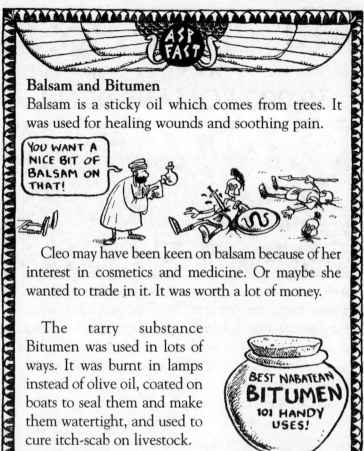

Balsam and Bitumen

Balsam is a sticky oil which comes from trees. It was used for healing wounds and soothing pain.

> YOU WANT A NICE BIT OF BALSAM ON THAT!

Cleo may have been keen on balsam because of her interest in cosmetics and medicine. Or maybe she wanted to trade in it. It was worth a lot of money.

The tarry substance Bitumen was used in lots of ways. It was burnt in lamps instead of olive oil, coated on boats to seal them and make them watertight, and used to cure itch-scab on livestock.

BEST NABATEAN **BITUMEN** 101 HANDY USES!

Through trade deals like this, there was more money coming into the coffers of Egypt than there had been for years.

She was going to need it. Antony's campaigns cost a lot of money. And Antony's campaigns weren't going very well. Here's how the Roman papers might have reported the Parthian campaign.

THE CENTURION

XX/V/DCCXVIII (36BC)

30,000 ROMANS DEAD!

Mark Antony's attempt to conquer Parthia has ended in chaos and defeat. The *Centurion* has received reports from Syria about the shambles which Antony calls a campaign.

Here's what his own soldiers say he did wrong. First, he set off too early in the year – because he wanted to get back to his girlfriend Cleo before next winter. Then he chose a steep and narrow route through the Armenian mountains into Parthia. This meant his baggage train was left behind and half the army had to stay behind and guard it.

'I wouldn't mind, but his own generals were warning him it wouldn't work,' said a veteran of twelve campaigns. 'If you ask me, he's lost his grip.'

Armenians strike

The King of Armenia crept up behind and attacked the rear of the Roman army – while the King of Parthia attacked the vanguard. 'It was a real trouncing. No point beating about the bush,' said the same seasoned vet.

150

Antony was forced to retreat – bringing disgrace on Rome's eagle standard. His baggage train was destroyed. Our boys limped back down rocky paths, starving, with no shoes, their clothes in rags. When the weather turned cold, they dropped dead like flies from wounds, chest complaints and gut-ache. 'There must be at least 30,000 men dead in this poxy campaign,' said another soldier.

Antony in despair

Antony knows he boobed. Sources close to him, who refuse to be named, say that he is close to suicide.

Nothing personal, but *The Centurion* thinks it might be the best thing for Rome if you did it, sir! You have brought enough disgrace on the Empire. Spare us more shame and take the honourable way out!

EAGLE FACT

Do or die

Romans were supposed to win battles or die in the attempt. Defeat was a disgrace. It was better to fall on your own sword than be defeated by an enemy. It was especially important not to be captured, because then your enemy would humiliate you – and Rome.

OUCH!

SPLOIK!

Antony didn't kill himself. He seems to have felt he had an obligation to his troops – who still idolized him, despite everything – to get them back to safety. So he headed for Syria and set up camp there with what remained of his army. Desperate, he wrote to Cleopatra, asking her to come and bring clothing for his troops and money to pay them.

Cleo didn't rush to his side. No one knows why. Maybe it was because she had just had another baby – little Ptolemy Philadelphus, called after the most successful Ptolemy of all. Maybe it was because Cleo didn't like losers. She certainly didn't like parting with money.

Antony knew this. He was really worried that she was going to ditch him. Here's what Plutarch says:

He became distraught and took to heavy drinking. He could not endure the waiting but would jump up from the table to look for her arrival. At last, she came by sea with large quantities of clothing and money, though some accounts say that she came with clothing only, and that Antony got money from his own private funds to distribute to the soldiers as if it were a gift from her.

Meanwhile, back in Rome. . .

While Antony had been losing campaigns and men in Parthia, Octavian was doing rather well. 'After prolonged unrest, he restored peace by land and sea,' said an official inscription in the Forum in Rome.

Octavian was a strong efficient ruler. He modelled himself on the Greek god, Apollo, who was the god of reason and order. He had the head of Apollo engraved on his coins – whereas Antony's Roman coins showed Dionysus, the wild god of wine and revelry.

Octavian was every bit as ambitious as Antony and Cleopatra. He wanted to rule the whole Roman Empire too, both east and west. And he hated the way Antony had behaved towards his sister. He had left her pregnant when he went back to Cleopatra, and now she was bringing up four children on her own – the two she had with Antony and Antony's two sons from his marriage to Fulvia.

However, even though Antony had behaved badly towards her, Octavia was a loyal wife. If it came to war between Antony and Octavian, Octavia would be on her husband's side. Octavian didn't want to fight against his sister, so he held back from going to war with Antony. In fact, he even sent some men and supplies for the army Octavia was getting together to help Antony make a second attack on Parthia.

Antony panicked when he heard Octavia was on her way to help him. He felt bad about her, but he knew there was no hope of them getting back together. Plus it was going to be very awkward if she arrived with Cleo there.

DEAR OCTAVIA,

THANK YOU FOR TRYING TO HELP, BUT THIS IS NOT THE RIGHT TIME OR THE RIGHT PLACE FOR US TO GET TOGETHER. I DO NOT WANT TO BE THE CAUSE OF TROUBLE BETWEEN YOU AND YOUR BROTHER. PLEASE GO BACK TO ROME AND LOOK AFTER THE CHILDREN.

LOVE,
ANTONY

PS IF YOU REALLY WANT TO HELP, PLEASE SEND THE SHIPS AND PROVISIONS ON TO ME. THEY WILL BE VERY WELCOME.

Octavian wasn't ready to attack Antony at that point. And at the last minute, Antony couldn't face another difficult Parthian campaign. Instead he decided to have a go at the King of Armenia. The King of Armenia was just a tiddler, but he'd helped to defeat Antony. Antony went to teach him a lesson. He conquered Armenia, and brought the King and his two sons back to Cleopatra as prisoners.

What shall we wear?

Antony and Cleopatra celebrated Antony's return to Alexandria as if he had won the most enormous victory. They decided to put on a Roman Triumph in Alexandria. As always, Cleo made it into a star-spangled spectacular, and dressed her children specially for the occasion.

Alexander, 9, her eldest son by Antony, was all dressed up as the King of Media in a long robe, with a high narrow hat with tiara and a peacock feather.

Little Ptolemy Philadelphus, 2, was dressed as a Macedonian prince with long boots, a short purple cloak, and a broad-brimmed hat with a diadem for a hat-band.

No one says what Caesarion was wearing, but it was

155

probably Egyptian robes. And poor old Cleopatra Selene wasn't even there, as far as we can tell. Maybe her mum thought one successful woman in the family was enough.

Mum herself was decked out as the goddess Isis (again). This meant a long, swirling rainbow-coloured dress, a black cloak, a head-dress with a moon and a serpent on her head, and lots of jewellery.

Cleo sat on a golden throne in a platform in the gymnasium, with her children standing around her. Beside her was an even bigger golden throne, empty and waiting for Antony.

He was marching at the head of his troops, through the streets of Alexandria. He was in Roman gear. Although he liked lounging about in Egyptian robes, his men didn't like to see it. They thought it meant he had 'gone native'.

Behind Antony walked the King of Armenia and his two sons, weighed down by chains of solid gold. Ant was about to present them as a gift to Cleopatra. That wasn't his only present for Cleo and sons that day. When he took his seat beside her, it was just the start of a big ceremony. By the end, everyone was much more important than they had been at the beginning.

Cleo was Queen of Egypt, Cyprus, Libya and part of Syria, with her son Caesarion as her consort. Antony crowned her Queen of Kings. Nine-year-old Alexander was crowned King of Armenia, Media and Parthia. Two-year-old Ptol was crowned King of Phoenicia, the rest of Syria and Cilicia.

When the coronation was over, he and Alex kissed their parents, before marching off with guards of honour.

And for my next trick . . .

To celebrate the great occasion there was yet another new coin.

On top of the world

Without herself fighting a single battle, Cleopatra had won huge tracts of land for herself and her children. She had the VPR in charge of the Eastern Empire in love with her and firmly on her side. And she could also claim the right to rule in Rome through Caesarion, her son by Julius Caesar.

CLEOPATRA IS TOP QUEEN!
CAME TO THE THRONE WITHOUT A BEAN,
NOW SHE'S LOADED, AS WE'VE SEEN.
CLEVER CLEOPATRA!

QUEENS ARE NEVER SAFE FROM FOES,
LOADED ONES ARE FIRST TO GO,
OCTAVIAN WANTS YOUR DOSH YOU KNOW.
WATCH OUT, CLEOPATRA!

The stele writers were right. Octavian and his supporters were just waiting their chance to have a go at her. It was at this time that they started putting around really nasty rumours about her. They said she had endless boyfriends. They said that she'd robbed Antony of his manliness and turned him into a woman.

Anything and everything was OK if it could be turned into propaganda against Cleopatra. Octavian even went to the Vestal Virgins and forced them to give him Anthony's will.

EAGLE FACT

The Vestal Virgins? Who they?
Vesta was the Roman goddess of the hearth. The hearth was the fireplace, the most important part of the home. In Rome there was a temple to Vesta with a sacred fireplace, symbolizing the hearth or centre of the Roman Empire. In it was a fire that never went out. Six unmarried girls looked after it.

You could became a Vestal Virgin anytime between the ages of six and ten. Then that was it. It was your job until you retired 30 years later.

The Romans left their wills and other important documents in the care of the Vestal Virgins, who were supposed to keep them safe and never ever read or show them to anyone until the person died.

So when Octavian snuck the will from them, it was Foul Play. He didn't care. In fact, he read bits of it to the Senate because he knew these would really shock his fellow Romans.

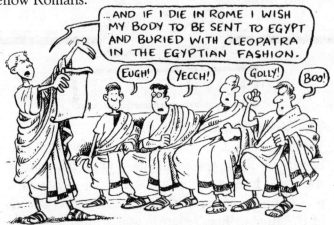

The Roman Senators thought this was awful. The Egyptians mummified their dead, and shut them up in tombs. The Romans preferred a nice cremation which left no mess. To them the will was another sign that Antony had turned his back on Rome and 'gone native'.

Most important of all, Octavian and his mates told the Roman people that Antony and Cleopatra were planning to take over the Roman Empire and rule it from the East. They said that Rome itself would just be a tiny province in Egypt's huge empire.

The Roman people didn't like the sound of that. They turned on Antony's friends. Fighting broke out once more and Antony's supporters had to flee for their lives.

ANTONY AND CLEO VERSUS ROME

Now it was only a matter of time before Octavian and Antony went to war. Octavian was in no hurry. He knew that Antony couldn't invade Italy, because the Roman soldiers under his command wouldn't wear it. They weren't going to invade their own country in the name of the Egyptian Queen.

The Egyptian army wasn't much cop, but the Egyptians had always been good sailors, so Cleo decided to prepare a great fleet to fight for Antony.

AND REMEMBER WHAT FUN WE HAD LAST TIME WE WENT SAILING?

ULP!

She was very efficient at this sort of thing. She arranged for the ships to be built in the Lebanon, using cedar wood from the forests. Because the organization of the docks there was not reliable enough for her, she put them under

Egyptian supervision. Cleopatra had 500 vast ships built, which were a cross between castles and battering-rams.

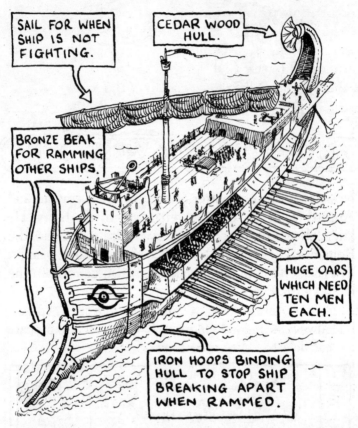

SAIL FOR WHEN SHIP IS NOT FIGHTING.

CEDAR WOOD HULL.

BRONZE BEAK FOR RAMMING OTHER SHIPS.

HUGE OARS WHICH NEED TEN MEN EACH.

IRON HOOPS BINDING HULL TO STOP SHIP BREAKING APART WHEN RAMMED.

Building the ships wasn't the end of it. Cleo also had to organize food, clothes and transport for all the thousands of men involved in the war. This she did, practically single-handed, because Antony was depressed and drinking heavily. Everyone was paid, everyone fed. This in itself was quite unusual in wartime.

Despite this efficiency, the Romans under Antony

were unhappy. They wanted to fight on land. They thought Antony was only fighting at sea because he was doing what Cleopatra told him. Some of his oldest friends decided to run away. One of these was Ahenobarbus, a real Roman soldier, who served with Antony through thick and thin. Here is a note that Ahenobarbus might have written at the time.

IT'S NO GOOD. THE BOSS AIN'T THE BOSS ANY MORE. I MEAN, I LIKE A DRINK AS WELL AS THE NEXT MAN, BUT THIS IS RIDICULOUS. ANT'S OUT OF IT, MORNING, NOON AND NIGHT. SHE'S THE ONE WEARING THE TOGA.

I'M NO FAN OF OCTAVIAN, BUT AT LEAST HE'S ROMAN. HER, SHE'S EGYPTIAN. OR GREEK OR WHATEVER. SHE AIN'T ROMAN, ANYWAY. I CAN'T GO FIGHTING MY OWN PEOPLE FOR HER.

IT'S GOING TO BE ANOTHER PARTHIA, IF YOU ASK ME. I MEAN, EVEN RATS HAVE GOT MORE SENSE THAN TO STAY ON BOARD A SINKING SHIP.

IT BREAKS MY HEART TO LEAVE HIM, BUT THERE'S NOTHING ELSE I CAN DO. BETTER TO SHIFT OVER TO OCTAVIAN NOW, BEFORE THE DEFEAT. HE'S MORE LIKELY TO GIVE ME A JOB. I'VE GOT MY FAMILY TO THINK ABOUT AFTER ALL. A MAN'S GOT TO EAT.

I WISH IT HADN'T COME TO THIS.

Ahenobarbus stole away in the dead of night, leaving everything he owned behind him.

Antony was very sad when he heard what had happened. He loved Ahenobarbus as much as Ahenobarbus loved him. He knew if good men were leaving him, it was the beginning of the end. Nevertheless, he was a generous man. Without telling Cleopatra, who would have been furious, he sent all Ahenobarbus's possessions and servants after him.

The next guy who tried it wasn't a big friend of Antony's. He was captured trying to leave and executed to make sure no one else followed.

Still men left. And those who stayed weren't happy. Over and over again, people tried to persuade Antony that he must leave the Queen behind when he went to war. Romans did not like fighting under a woman, and they were starting to feel that this woman was very unlucky. It was also becoming clear that there were not nearly enough sailors to man the huge ships.

Ready, steady. . .

Over in Italy, Octavian was also preparing for war. He didn't have chests and chests of gold. He had to raise his funds through taxes. It took time and it wasn't popular. The one thing he had going for him was that he knew Antony couldn't invade Italy, which gave him a breathing space.

His admiral, Agrippa, knew what Cleopatra was up to with her navy. He decided not to try and compete with her big ships – for one thing, Octavian couldn't afford it. Instead, he ordered lots of fast little ships to be built, the sort that pirates used. Unlike Cleopatra's huge hulks, they could be manned by fewer sailors, and could change direction quickly.

Get the goddess on your side!

Finally Octavian was ready. He went to the temple of Bellona, the Roman goddess of war. She had snakes for hair. She was dressed in armour covered in blood, and she carried a blood-stained whip above her head. She was so frightening that her temple was kept locked most of the time for fear she would get out.

Now Octavian wanted her out. He wanted her to kill Antony. He went and flung the temple doors open wide. He sacrificed a wild boar to the goddess. Then he came out of the temple and yelled at the top of his lungs. . .

Then he set sail with his nippy little fleet from Italy.

165

War!!!

WE'RE ALL GOING ON A... SUMMER WAR-A-DAY,
NO MORE RULING FOR A... WEEK OR TWO,
WE'RE ALL GOING ON A SUMMER WAR-A-DAY,
TO MAKE OUR DREAMS COME TRUE !

Poor old Roman soldiers. They never got to go on a proper holiday. Instead, summer meant another campaign. Sure, you might march to some interesting places, even see some good beaches, but you also stood a good chance of getting injured or dying in battle.

Octavian and Antony spent the whole of the summer of 31 BC fighting each other. A lot of men were killed; a lot of ships were sunk, including 270 of Cleopatra's great hulks. By the end of the summer, Octavian had the Egyptian navy trapped in a bay at a place in Greece called Actium.

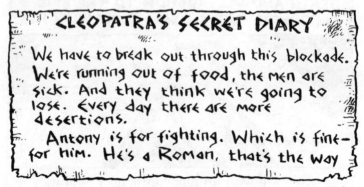

CLEOPATRA'S SECRET DIARY

We have to break out through this blockade. We're running out of food, the men are sick. And they think we're going to lose. Every day there are more desertions.

Antony is for fighting. Which is fine—for him. He's a Roman, that's the way he thinks. It's honour, honour, honour all the time with him. But my job is to make sure my treasure doesn't fall into Octavian's hands. If I can get that safely back to Egypt, then we're home and dry. If, on the other hand, O gets the treasure, then we really have had it.

I have told Antony my plan. We come out, as if to fight. There's a good chance we'll defeat O. Ant is a far better general. But just in case, I'm bringing my sails. I've told him he should do the same

As always, Cleopatra was full of common sense. For the Romans, however, it was very important to win a great victory. They didn't believe in 'flee and fight another day'.

Antony's Roman advisers were thinking in terms of a Roman battle. They don't seem to have been aware of Cleo's plan. It spooked them that she was insisting on coming along to the battle aboard her own, smaller ship. It spooked them even more when they heard Antony was taking sails on board his ships. Usually ships' sails were left behind during sea battles. They were not needed during battle, when ships rammed each other, or grappled alongside each other for men to fight hand to hand. If Antony was taking them, it suggested that he secretly thought he might have to sail away in a hurry.

He did. The Battle of Actium was a mess from Antony's point of view. Octavian's ships were fast and well-manned. They were able to dart up to the vast floating castles, attack, and get out of the way.

This is how Plutarch describes what happened next:

Then Cleopatra's squadron of 60 ships was suddenly seen to hoist sail and make off from the very midst of the fight. Stationed behind the heavy ships, this squadron plunged through their line and threw them into disorder, but with straining sails before the following wind, her ships set course for the Peloponnese.

Antony, aboard one of the big hulks, appears to have

been astonished. Maybe Cleopatra hadn't told him of Plan B. His own flagship was too huge and unwieldy to follow her, so he climbed aboard another smaller ship, and went chasing after Cleopatra.

Now Antony's men were fighting without their leader, who was scudding after the love of his life. They tried to manoeuvre the huge heavy ships she had built for them. The wind blew up, and the Roman ships were able to dive in among them. By four in the afternoon, it was all over. Antony's men had surrendered.

169

That night those huge ships burned on the water. Their bronze beaks had been hacked off. They would be used to make a monument to the Octavian victory.

When Antony caught up with Cleopatra, it was not a happy reunion.

CLEOPATRA'S SECRET DIARY

2 days after Actium

Ant still sulking. Won't speak to me. For two days now he's sat in the prow of the ship with his head in his hands.

I expect it's all about his honour. Romans aren't supposed to run away, all that stuff. So stupid. What's the point of staying to fight if you know you're going to get beaten?

3 days after Actium

Am worried sick about Antony. I think he might throw himself overboard. He's still not eating and he won't even look at me. I guess it's deserting his men that's getting to him. But if we'd all tried to flee Octavian would have come after us.

6 days after Actium

Made it up with Antony, more or less, but I've never seen him so depressed. He says he's finished, and he blames me.

I keep telling him I can build another fleet any time he wants. He says what's the point? No Roman will ever want to fight for him again, and he can't hold Egypt with just Egyptians, he said. I think he may be right.

Soon news reached them that their fleet had been completely destroyed. At this point Antony roused himself. He took one of Cleopatra's treasure ships and offered it to all the soldiers with him, telling them to take the treasure, leave him, and make peace with Octavian. Men stood around with tears in their eyes, unwilling to do what he said but knowing there was no alternative.

Yes, Cleo sailed back into Alexandria with garlands on the bows of her ships, as if she had won the Battle of Actium. She knew she was only as strong as people thought she was. And after all, she hadn't lost her land, or her treasure. The important thing now was to make sure there weren't any risings against her.

Antony wasn't with her. He just couldn't face it. He'd gone ashore at a place called Cyrene, across the Egyptian border. He wandered about in the desert for a bit. By the time he turned up in Alexandria, Cleo had a new plan.

Now what?

King Malchus of Nabataea (the one who lost all his bitumen to Cleo) soon received a letter from a friend...

Dear Malk,

Thought you would like to know that Queen C. is having what remains of her navy hauled overland to the shores of the Red Sea. Seems her plan is to escape with Antony and go and live in India. Unless, of course, something happens to the boats in the meantime.

Your ever loyal tip-off merchant, P

It gave him an idea.

CLEOPATRA'S SECRET DIARY

Curses on Malchus! His Arabs have set fire to all my ships! They've burnt every last one to ashes. So that's put the lid on the India idea.

Meanwhile, Antony is being absolutely impossible. He's built himself a little house out by the lighthouse where he sits and mopes all day long.

SNIFFLE

Meanwhile, back in Rome, Octavian wasn't having it all his own way, either.

THE CENTURION
XIV/I/DCCXXIV (30 BC)

'NO WAR WITHOUT PAY'

Octavian's new plans to conquer Egypt hit a rock last night – when the army came out on strike.

Feelings are running high against Octavian because soldiers loyal to Rome have still not been paid – while Antony's men arrive home laden with gold coins, plate and jewels.

Octavian met with strikers' leaders last night to explain his position. 'It's not so easy in a republic,' he told them. 'You have to raise the money through taxes – and there's never enough. If we had captured the Egyptian treasure ship, we wouldn't be in this position. One more campaign, we'll get that treasure. And then I'll pay you.'

The men were not convinced. They want their pay before they fight – and Occo hasn't got it.

CLEOPATRA'S SECRET DIARY

At last Antony is bored with living like a hermit. He's back in the palace, and I've arranged a whole string of parties to cheer him up and make him think of something other than Octavian.

The fact is, Octavian isn't coming after us, whatever Ant says. He can't afford to. So, as I said to Ant— let's have a good time. The first big bash is to celebrate the coming of age of Caesarion – and Antony and Fulvia's eldest son Antyllus, of course.

Then the plan is to send Antyllus over to visit Octavian, with a nice little present. After all, it's money Octavian's after. That's all Rome's ever wanted from Egypt, so if I give him the money, he won't have to fight for it, will he?

Antyllus was sent to Rome, as Cleo planned. He took with him a large sum of money, which Octavian pocketed without making any promises that he would back off. Antyllus came back saying things didn't look good. Cleo realized she couldn't win. She wrote a letter to Octavian:

174

Most Noble Triumvir Octavian

Cleopatra Thea, Queen of Egypt, Cyprus and Syria, sends you greetings and hopes you are in good health.

Look, I'm getting a bit tired of this queen lark, and I know you don't like me much, so how about I abdicate? I'm happy to go, on two conditions.

1. You let my children rule in my place.

2. You let Antony and me live out our days quietly as private citizens.

This is going to save us both a lot of grief, so I look forward to hearing from you as soon as possible.

ΚΛΕΟΠΑΤΡΑ

Octavian ignored this. There was no way he was going to let Antony live.

However, he hadn't ruled out doing some sort of deal with Cleopatra. He sent a messenger to speak to her – a very handsome, charming man, whom he thought Cleopatra might fall for.

175

Behind closed doors

Cleopatra spent a long time talking to this messenger. No one knows exactly what went on between them, but it seems likely that the messenger was offering Cleo a deal. Get rid of Antony and Octavian will look kindly on you.

By 'get rid of' the messenger meant *either* execute him *or* banish him.

So why did it take so long? After all, Cleo loved Antony, didn't she? Surely it wouldn't have taken more than a minute to say NO, NO, NO.

Cleo the woman did love Antony. She found him pretty trying at times, what with his sulking and drinking, but she loved his generosity and his courage and the way he dreamt the same dreams she did.

On the other hand, Cleo the Queen had chosen Antony because he was a Very Powerful Roman and could help Egypt. Now he wasn't a VPR any more. He couldn't help Egypt – but Octavian was a VPR and Octavian could. The only trouble was she didn't trust Octavian.

No wonder Cleo dithered, and played for time.

In the end she spent so long with the messenger that Antony got suspicious. He thought they were flirting. He had the guy whipped and sent back to Octavian.

CLEOPATRA'S SECRET DIARY

A close shave today. That handsome messenger nearly had me convinced that Octavian would forgive everything if only I handed Ant over to him.

As if. All O wants is my treasure. And he's not getting it, not without giving me something back. I've given orders for it all to be taken to the monument. I'm storing it on the ground floor, with firewood stacked up all round it.

Then if O invades the whole lot goes up in flames. That'll teach him.

In July that year, Octavian invaded Egypt. Antony was quite pleased. Now he had a chance to fight, and with any luck he would be killed in battle.

Antony was so cheered up by the prospect that he won the first battle. At that, he became very cocksure. He sent a message to Octavian.

OCTAVIAN,

HOW ABOUT YOU AND ME SETTLE THIS WHOLE THING BETWEEN OURSELVES? SINGLE COMBAT? IT WOULD SAVE A FEW LIVES. LET ME KNOW WHEN AND WHERE.

YOURS,

ANTONY

Octavian must have laughed. Why would he risk fighting Antony single-handed, when Antony had nothing to lose?

DEAR ANTONY,

GET LOST. I HAVE BETTER WAYS OF DYING. SEE YOU ON THE BATTLEFIELD.

OCTAVIAN

The eve of the invasion

HARK, HARK, DIONYSUS IS LEAVING
DID YOU HEAR HIM RUN THROUGH THE STREETS LAST NIGHT?
DID YOU HEAR THE SINGING, THE GHOSTLY WAILING, AND NO ONE THERE? DID YOU GET A FRIGHT?

Lots of people reported strange sounds in Alexandria on the night before Octavian marched on the city. They said it sounded as if wild party-goers were running through the streets and out towards Octavian's camp. They read deep meanings into it. They said the god Dionysus was abandoning the city. Antony worshipped Dionysus, so if his god was leaving him, he was doomed.

I KNOW WHEN TO LEAVE A PARTY!

ALEX-ANDRIA

Next morning, Antony sent all his soldiers and sailors to their posts to guard the city. An hour later, no one was there. His men knew a loser when they saw one.

179

They went over to Octavian, in such numbers that Antony was convinced that Cleopatra had arranged it. He thought she was in league with Octavian. He flew into a rage. He roared his way through the city, raging that it was all the Queen's fault.

And so her servants ran to him and told Antony exactly that. Plutarch describes how he received the news...

Not doubting this message for a moment, he said to himself, 'Fate has taken away my only joy and reason for living.' Then he said, 'O Cleopatra, your death does not hurt me for I shall soon join you, but you put me to shame, for it seems I have less courage and nobility than a woman.'

He then turned to his loyal servant Eros. Eros had always promised his master that he would kill him if ever Antony asked. But now the moment had come, Eros couldn't do it. He drew his sword, but instead of killing Antony, he turned it towards himself and fell on it.

Now Antony tried to kill himself.

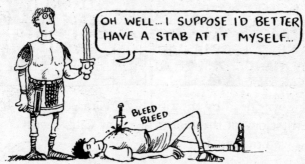

OH WELL... I SUPPOSE I'D BETTER HAVE A STAB AT IT MYSELF...

BLEED BLEED

He made a mess of it. He stabbed himself, but he didn't die. Badly wounded, bleeding, in pain, he begged his friends to finish him off, but they all ran away. Someone must have told Cleopatra what had happened, for it wasn't long before her secretary Diomedes appeared with orders to bring him to the monument.

By the time they got him there, Octavian's troops were entering the city, so Cleo didn't dare unlock the doors. Instead, she had Antony hoisted up through an upper window of the monument. She herself had to help with this, puffing and groaning under his weight.

When they got him into the monument, they laid him on a bed, and she covered him with one of her own dresses. Cleopatra was crazy with grief by this time. She tore her hair and beat her breast. Antony tried to comfort her, advising her to seek safety and telling her which of Octavian's men she could trust.

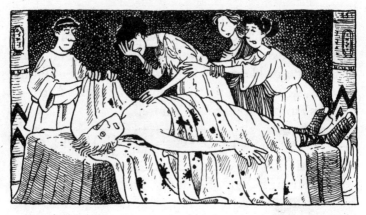

He was dead by the time Octavian got there. It was the first day of the month we now call August, in the year we now call 30 BC.

But what about the treasure?

Proculeius was one of the people Antony had told Cleo she could trust, but she didn't trust him much. She spoke to him through a grating. She promised she would abdicate, but only on condition her children were allowed to rule in her place. Proculeius pretended to think this was a good idea. He said he was going to go and tell Octavian what she had said, but he was back in no time with a group of soldiers. He had spotted the open window through which Antony had been hauled into the building. The soldiers climbed through the window and took possession of the monument.

Cleo tried to stab herself, but they managed to stop her and took her away.

CLEOPATRA'S SECRET DIARY

I have nothing now. Nothing. Antony is dead and Octavian has all my treasure. Egypt is finished. I wish I were dead.

A few days later Cleo was taken before Octavian. He had all the power now. He didn't have to give her anything at all, and she knew it. Her foreign policy – to keep the most powerful Roman of the day in love with her – had hit an obstacle. It would never work with the cool-headed, cold-hearted Octavian.

All the same, Cleopatra did have something that Octavian wanted. He wanted her alive, to walk in his Roman Triumph as her sister Arsinoe had done in Julius Caesar's so many years before. It would be quite something to see the proud Queen of Egypt walking through the streets of Rome, clanking her chains.

Cleopatra persuaded Octavian that she would do anything he wanted, provided he allowed her to visit the monument one last time, in order to pay her last respects to Antony, who had been buried there. Before she went she asked her lady-in-waiting to do her a favour.

> To the Figman,
> Please send a large basket of ripe figs AS DISCUSSED for the Queen. It should reach the monument no later than this evening.
>
> Yours, Charmian
> (Lady-in-waiting to Queen Cleopatra)

Cleopatra's doctor wrote about what happened next and Plutarch put it into his account:

*So Cleopatra mourned Antony, and crowned his urn
with garlands and kissed it. Then she ordered a bath to
be made ready, and coming from the bath, she rested
and was served a most sumptuous meal. Now while she
was at dinner, a countryman came to her bringing a
basket. When the guards stopped him and demanded to
see what was in it, he pulled away some of the leaves
and showed ripe figs which looked so good the soldiers
were tempted to eat them. Then they allowed him to
take the fruit to the Queen. After she had dined,
Cleopatra took a tablet and wrote on it for Octavian,
and sealed it and sent it. Then she dismissed all but her
two faithful waiting-women and closed the doors of the
monument.*

Cleo's message was that she wanted to be buried with
Antony. As soon as he read it, Octavian knew what it
meant. He sent his people to the monument to stop
Cleopatra. They were too late.

*At the monument the guards had seen nothing wrong,
but when all the people burst through the doors they
found Cleopatra dead upon a golden couch, dressed in
her royal robes. One of her women, who was called Iras,
was dead at her feet, while the other, Charmian,
tottering, hardly able to stand, was trying to put straight
the diadem on Cleopatra's head. One of the guards cried
angrily, 'Charmian, is this well done?' And the woman
answered, 'Very well done, and fitting for a princess
descended from so many kings.' Uttering these words,
she fell down dead by the side of the couch.*

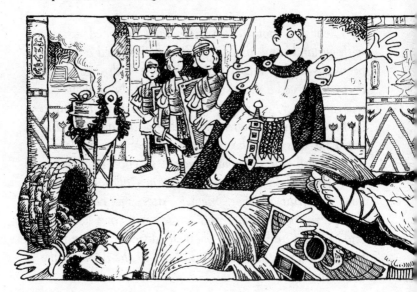

What did they die of?

No one is quite sure. Most people think Cleo and her ladies died of poisonous snake bites. It's thought there were snakes hidden in the basket of figs, although no snake was ever found.

What *is* known is that Cleo knew all about quick and painless ways of dying. She had made a study of it. And in her dying, she was as quick and efficient as she had been in everything else she had done in life.

To be killed by a snake fitted perfectly with her image as goddess-queen. Remember the sacred snakes of Egypt on her crown? They had guarded her in life, and now by killing her, they were taking her where Octavian could never harm her.

Cleo refused to live as a defeated queen. Instead she preferred to die as she had lived – dressed to kill, in a gesture which all her people would understand. She

died, dressed in the royal robes of Isis, a goddess to the end. That is how she wanted people to remember her.

ASP FACT

Mercy Killing
Criminals in Alexandria were sometimes allowed to die by cobra bite because it causes a quick and painless death.

187

In those days, you smashed all the statues of your enemy when you conquered him or her. With Cleo's death, Octavian set his soldiers loose in Egypt. Soon there wasn't a statue of Antony left standing. However, he gave orders that none of the statues of Cleopatra should be touched. Don't think it was out of the goodness of his heart. It was money again. One of Cleopatra's supporters had paid him a huge sum to leave them alone.

And Octavian granted Cleo her last wish. She was buried beside her Antony. In the words of Shakespeare's play, 'No grave on earth shall clip in it a pair so famous'.

WHO KILLED OUR QUEEN?
I, SAID YOUNG CAESAR,
I JUST MEANT TO
TEASE HER,
I KILLED YOUR QUEEN.

WHO BROUGHT THE SNAKE?
I, SAID THE FARMER,
I JUST WANTED TO
CALM HER,
I BROUGHT THE SNAKE.

WHO SAW THEM DIE?
I, SAID THE FLY,
ALONE, NO ONE BY,
I SAW THEM DIE.

BUT THE TALE OF HER LIFE
AND THE TALE OF HER DEATH
WILL BE RETOLD FOR EVER
WHILE MEN STILL HAVE
BREATH.

AFTER CLEOPATRA

Whatever happened to. . .?

Egypt
She was now a Roman province, without a king of her own, and the 'breadbasket' of Rome. From then on, Egypt became the main supplier of food for the city of Rome. Centuries later, when the Roman Empire was just a memory, Egypt was invaded by Arabs. Today Egypt is a Muslim country.

Alexandria
It's still a port, but no longer capital of Egypt. The famous library with all its rare and precious books was burned to the ground by Christian mobs in the fourth century. (They were a bigoted bunch – they didn't like all the books by non-Christian thinkers and philosophers.) The famous Pharos lighthouse was still working a thousand years after Cleo – but in the 11th century there was a terrible earthquake which toppled it for ever.

189

The River Nile
It went on flooding every year, right up until this
century. Then, in the 1960s, the Aswan Dam was built,
to control the flow of the river. It's done that – but the
land is not as fertile now the river brings no silt. And
the crocodiles are all stuck behind the Aswan Dam.
They still kill people south of the dam, but most of the
Nile is a crocodile-free zone.

Cleopatra's children
Caesarion was executed by Octavian. The twins and baby
Ptol walked as prisoners in Octavian's Triumph. Then
they were sent to live with Octavia, Ant's abandoned
wife. Cleopatra-Selene married King Juba of Mauretania.
No one knows what happened to the boys.

Antony's children
Both Antyllus and Ant's younger son, Iullus, were
executed - Antyllus for supporting his dad and Iullus for
getting too friendly with Octavian's daughter. Antony's
daughters, on the other hand, survived and became the
mothers and grandmothers of future Roman emperors.

And finally . . . Octavian

Having defeated Antony, he became Emperor of Rome. In fact his surname, Caesar, came to mean emperor. He called himself Augustus Caesar, which means an emperor so great, so important, he was more than human. Wonder where he got that idea from?

Augustus Caesar lived a long time, and became a strong emperor – but he never forgot Cleopatra. She had been too big a threat to the Roman way of life. He named the month in which he defeated her August, after himself, to mark his victory.

ONE LAST ASP FACT

Cleo's cash

Egypt's treasure made Italy safe for Octavian-Augustus to rule. He used it to pay off his debts, pay his soldiers, and give every Roman citizen a victory bonus. Interest rates in Rome fell from 12% to 4%. Without all the money Cleo had stashed away, Octavian would never have held on to his throne.

LOOK DEAR! IT'S OUR VICTORY BONUS!

So there you have it – the life of Clever Cleo and her Asp. The young girl who had come to the throne when Egypt was bankrupt had not only managed to stay queen against all the odds – she had made Egypt rich again, and she was popular with the people.

She was world-famous in her own time and she has gone on being world-famous to this day. Down the centuries, men and women have been fascinated by her. Thousands of words have been written, hundreds of portraits painted, there have been plays and films and songs about her and she's always popping up at fancy dress parties. (In fact, Lady Diana Cooper, a rich aristocrat, thought it was such fun to be Cleopatra that in the 1950s she used a photo of herself got up as Cleo in her passport!)

All in all, after all these years, Cleo's name still means GLAMOUR! WEALTH! POWER! SEX APPEAL! No wonder she goes on and on fascinating us. She really is HORRIBLY FAMOUS!

SO THERE!

Index

194

LOOK OUT FOR

→

LEONARDO
DA VINCI
WHAT A MASTERPIECE!
A STROKE OF GENIUS
Michael Cox

ELIZABETH I

I'M A CHOP OFF
THE OLD BLOCK!

REIGNS SUPREME

Margaret Simpson

MARY
QUEEN OF SCOTS
QUEEN, 18, SEEKS UNSUITABLE HUSBAND...
LONELY HEARTS
BORN TO RULE
Margaret Simpson

SHAKESPEARE
ALLOW ME TO PRESENT MY BOTTOM!
HIS DRAMATIC ACTS
Andrew Donkin

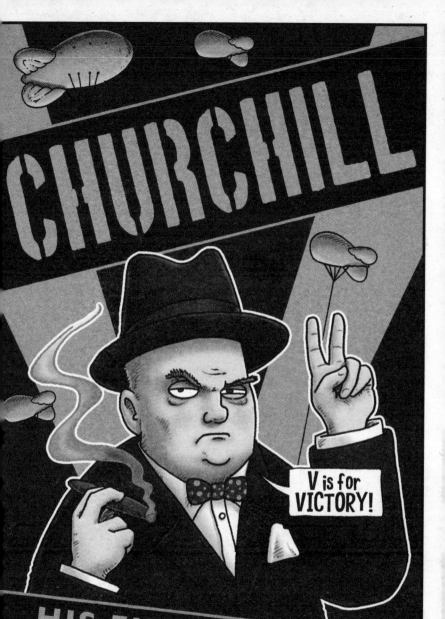